REMEMBER GOLIAD

Col. James Fannin, commander of the Texas forces at Goliad. Painting by Charles B. Normann.

REMEMBER GOLIAD
THEIR SILENT TENTS

By

Clifford Hopewell

EAKIN PRESS ★ Austin, Texas

Friends of the
Houston Public Library

itxry

FIRST EDITION

Published in the United States of America
By Eakin Press
A Division of Sunbelt Media, Inc.
P.O. Box 90159
Austin, Texas 78709
email: eakinpub@sig.net

2 3 4 5 6 7 8 9

ISBN 1-57168-195-7

Library of Congress Cataloging-in-Publication Data

*This book is dedicated to
Joshua, Bruce II, John, Jessie,
Jordan, Clay, and Jody.*

Presidio La Bahía near Goliad, 1895.
— Courtesy James H. Sutton, Jr., San Antonio,
from UT Institute of Texan Cultures.

Presidio La Bahía, 1997.

—From the author's files.

Some of the battlefield and graveyard on Coleto Plains, Goliad.

—From the author's files.

CONTENTS

Preface vii
1. War Begins 1
2. A Provisional Government is Formed 9
3. Dreams of Glory 18
4. On To Matamoros 26
5. Santa Anna Marches 32
6. Cast of Characters 39
7. Dreams of Glory Vanish 47
8. Garrison Life 55
9. The Gathering Storm 64
10. The Alamo Falls 73
11. Fannin Splits His Forces 82
12. Action At Refugio 90
13. Fannin Moves At Last 95
14. The Battle of Coleto Plains 101
15. In Captivity 111
16. Treachery and Execution 119
17. The Final Tally 129
18. The Summing Up 141
Epilogue 147
Notes 153
Bibliography 160
Index 163

Aerial view of Presidio La Bahía, Goliad.

—From author's files.

PREFACE

It was Palm Sunday, March 27, 1836, and it turned out to be the blackest day in the War for Independence between Texas and Mexico. It was the day that Col. James Walker Fannin, Jr., and his men were ruthlessly slaughtered at Presidio La Bahía, near the little town of Goliad, on the direct order of Gen. Antonio López de Santa Anna y Perez de Lebrón, president and dictator of Mexico.

In Goliad, only a few hundred yards from the fortress at La Bahía, which Fannin named Fort Defiance, there is a granite memorial erected in memory of those executed on that Palm Sunday morning. Although there are 342 names inscribed, it is possible there were actually more. The exact number of dead may never be known.

It had been scarcely a dozen years since the Mexican government authorized Stephen F. Austin and other empresarios to bring in settlers to colonize the Texas portion of the joint state of Coahuila-Texas. Now Mexico and the Texas portion of Coahuila-Texas were at war.

Perhaps war between the Anglo colonists and Mexico was inevitable, as there were so many differences between the two races. In addition to the vast cultural, social and economic differences, there were political and religious differences as well. Although the Mexican government in 1824 enacted laws designed to encourage newcomers to settle in Texas, at the same time it adopted a new federal constitution that prohibited any religious faith other than Roman Catholicism. Only Catholics could own property or practice law, and although the law was frequently ignored, it was still highly resented by the Protestant

Anglos. Trial by jury was revoked and in the distribution of land, preference would be given to Mexicans, although in many cases the Anglos were Mexican citizens. One clause of the constitution required the would-be colonist to appear before the local government and swear allegiance to the Mexican constitution. All this raised the hackles of the Anglo colonists.

There were many other differences. The Mexican government provided no schools for the children of the colonists. This, too, was resented by the Anglos, who had to build their own schools or send their children back to the United States to receive an education.

Although there were some marriages between the Anglos and the Mexicans, on the whole there was little social intermingling between the two groups. The average Mexican on his little plot of ground had no education, was dirt poor, and frequently his meals consisted of only beans and meal. Although some of the colonists were adventurers, many of them were highly educated men: lawyers and doctors welcome in the best homes back in the United States. Others were hard-working farmers and frontiersmen who had settled in this new territory in order to provide a better life for themselves and their families. They had far more energy and enterprise than their peasant Mexican neighbors. They grew crops on their farms; they raised cattle, and they ate well. They had virtually nothing in common with the Mexicans.

Gen. Anastasio Bustamante had taken office as president of Mexico on January 1, 1830. On April 6 a decree known as Bustamante's law went into effect and became the turning point in the relations of the Texas colonists and the government. The new law prohibited further American immigration into the colony, but encouraged the immigration of Europeans, particularly from Switzerland and Germany. In addition, the law proposed to settle Mexican convicts in Coahuila-Texas after their release from prison and military service, and peons were encouraged to settle there in return for land given them. New customs duties that restricted trade with other nations were imposed, and all land grants were suspended unless 100 colonists had already settled in the areas allotted.

Something was going to have to give.

Before serious hostilities broke out between the colonists and the Mexican government, there had been three previous attempts to declare Texas an independent nation. First, there had been the abortive Magee-Gutiérrez attempt in August 1812, while Mexico was still under the control of Spain. This was followed by the expedition led by Dr. James Long of Mississippi in the spring of 1819. This, too, proved unsuccessful. Finally, after Mexico had secured its own independence from Spain, there was the Fredonian Rebellion of December 1826, led by the two Edwards brothers. They declared their independence from Mexico and named their new territory the Republic of Fredonia, but their forces were quickly run out of the state.

The war that started in October 1835 proved to be the real thing. It is surprising how few volunteers who answered the call from Texas authorities had lived in the state for any period of time. Davy Crockett, a Texas hero, and his small band of followers from Tennessee had been in Texas only a few weeks when they perished at the Alamo. The majority of forces under Fannin's command at La Bahía had only crossed the borders into Texas a few months before they joined him, and although he had some mature and professional men in his ranks, by and large his troops consisted of young boys in their late teens and early twenties—many of them only fourteen or fifteen years of age. They came from such southern states as Louisiana, Mississippi, Tennessee, Alabama, Kentucky, and Georgia; there were some from Ohio and Maryland and even a few from Germany and Poland.

The fact that there were so few "Texans" in Fannin's army was a constant source of irritation to both Fannin and his men, and they all complained about it.

The war between Texas and Mexico was political to a high degree, between Mexican anti-Santa Anna forces, who wanted the law of 1824 upheld, and their opponents who supported both Santa Anna and the Bustamante law of 1830. A large number of those men were highly educated, cultured, and men of wealth and position. Many of them were sympathetic to the Texan cause until the Declaration of Independence from Mexico was announced; then, they could not go along with the idea of independence from their mother nation. Many Mexican leaders still supported the Texans.

Don Juan Martín de Veramendi, governor of Coahuila-Texas and Jim Bowie's father-in-law, sympathized with the Texans until he died in 1833. Among others who supported the colonists after the Declaration of Independence were Veramendi's brother-in-law, José Antonio Navarro, who was one of two native-born Texans who signed the Declaration of Independence, and José Francisco Ruiz, the first public schoolmaster of San Antonio. His son, Francisco Antonio Ruiz, was *alcalde* (mayor) of Bexar and, with Navarro, signed the declaration. Dr. Lorenzo de Zavala was a highly educated and cultured Mexican who fought at Gonzales to retain a six-pound cannon. When the Texans formed a provisional government, he was elected vice-president.

Capt. Placido Benavides was *alcalde* of Victoria and organized a company of thirty ranchers to reinforce the Texan army at the Battle of Bexar Dec. 5-9, 1835. He later served with Dr. Grant's foolish expedition to San Patricio and narrowly escaped with his life when Dr. Grant's forces were wiped out at Agua Dulce Creek.

One of Sam Houston's favorite scouts was Capt. Juan Nepomuceno Seguin, who performed yeoman service for both Houston and William Barret Travis. Seguin commanded forces of several dozen of his compatriots and he and his scouts served at the Battles of Concepción, Bexar and the Alamo, and at least six of his men were killed when the Alamo fell. Two of his scouts, Antonio Cruz y Arocha and Alejandro de la Garza, served as messengers to Fannin when Travis called for help.

A prominent Mexican merchant, José Cassiano, served as a scout along the Rio Grande and reported the movements of Santa Anna's army to the Texans.

Mariana Carajabal was a young Mexican in Fannin's army and was executed at Goliad.

Of the 188 men who died at the Alamo, seven were Mexicans born in San Antonio de Bexar, and one was born in Laredo.

In addition to the above, there were many Mexicans who, although they did not serve in the military, passed along valuable information to Texas commanders as Santa Anna and his various armies marched through Texas.

The War for Independence against Mexico lasted six and one-half months. There were many skirmishes and short campaigns, but only six major battles: the Battle of Gonzales, the Battle of Concepción, the Battle of San Antonio, the Battle of the Alamo, the Battle of Coleto Plains, and the Battle of San Jacinto. Four wins and two losses, and all of them were of short duration. The first major victory, the Battle of San Antonio, took four days. Although the Alamo had been under constant bombardment before it fell on the thirteenth day, the actual storming and taking of the fortress took only a number of hours. The actual fighting in the plains of Coleto lasted only several hours before the respective forces called it quits on account of darkness, and the next day Fannin surrendered. The final battle of the war at Buffalo Bayou, on the plains of San Jacinto, lasted just eighteen minutes. But that was the victory that counted as the Texans triumphed over Santa Anna and ended the war.

It might say something for the art of warfare that both losses of the Texans occurred while they were on the defensive, with one army being holed up in a fort, and four victories occurred when the Texans were on the attack.

Although this story mentions prominent personalities, incidents, and places of the Texas revolution, it is primarily the story of Col. James Walker Fannin, Jr., doomed commander of Fort Defiance, his lieutenants, and the men under his command at the Presidio La Bahía.

I have tried to keep the facts as accurate as I could track them down in my research. I hope there are no errors in this book; but if there are, as the author, I accept the sole responsibility.

Clifford Hopewell
Dallas, Texas

Monument with the names of persons executed at Goliad.
—From the author's files.

Victims of treachery's brutal stroke,
They died to break the tyrant's yoke,
On Fame's eternal camping ground,
Their silent tents are spread,
And glory guards with hallowed round
The bivouac of these dead.

—Inscription on Monument
at Coleto Battlefield

1

WAR BEGINS

On that fateful day of March 27, 1836, as the volleys were fired from the rifles of Santa Anna's *Santanistas* and the bodies of those executed fell to the ground, there were many among the witnesses whose eyes were filled with tears and sorrow. Among them were Joseph H. Spohn, whose life had been spared because the Mexicans used him as an interpreter. As Spohn watched the scene in shocked disbelief, his mind raced back to the days a few months previously when he and his friends left their native Alabama to fight for the Texan cause. Dr. Jack Shackelford, whose life was spared as he was a physician, looked on in sorrow and sadness as he saw the many young men he had personally recruited—including his own son and nephew—die virtually at his feet. Others watched in grim silence.

For some time there had been severe friction between the Anglo-American colonists in the Texas portion of the joint province of Coahuila-Texas and the Mexican government. The situation had become exacerbated since the Mexican congress had given President-General Santa Anna the powers of an absolute dictator. To secure his grip on Mexico, he promptly abolished the constitution and all state legislatures, including that of Coahuila-Texas, and virtually abolished the militia by decreeing that all states turn in their weapons to the central government. Worst of all—from the Anglo-American view—he announced that it was his intention to drive all Americans out of Texas and back into the United States.

The province of Zacatecas refused to acquiesce to Santa Anna and surrender their weapons. To show who was master, and to punish them for their impudence, the dictator placed himself at the head of his army and marched upon the province. After a bloody battle on May 11, 1835, his troops overwhelmed the Zacatecans, killing some 2,000 of them and taking 2,700 as prisoners.[1] Not satisfied, the victors marched into the capital and for the next two days engaged in butchering the unfortunate inhabitants and plundering their city.

When news of this atrocity reached the Texans they were dismayed, especially when they remembered Santa Anna's promise to drive them from Texas.

Prior to these happenings there had been several incidents that created rumblings of discontent. There was the hated "Bustamante's Law" of April 6, 1830,[2] and now the Mexican government had allocated half a million dollars to establish military posts at Anahuac, Velasco, Nacogdoches, San Antonio de Bexar, Goliad, and other points.

Anahuac was a small city at the mouth of the Trinity River, near Galveston Bay. Col. John Bradburn, an American adventurer from Kentucky, who had been in Mexico and Texas for a number of years and had fought against Spain, was appointed both military commander and customs collector of the town. It proved to be an unfortunate choice. Irascible, tactless and arbitrary, his pompousness made him a frequent butt of practical jokes and ridicule.

The high-handed Bradburn contributed to his growing unpopularity by commandeering supplies from his troops without payment, and using slave labor without compensation in the erection of military buildings. Further, he encouraged slaves to revolt against their masters.

William Barret (Buck) Travis, a fiery, red-haired twenty-six-year-old lawyer from South Carolina, had been in Texas as early as April 1831. Travis lived in Anahuac and attempted to recover two runaway slaves for his client, and soon found himself in

Bradburn's guardhouse along with a couple who had been imprisoned for no reason except they had played a practical joke on the colonel.

The outraged colonists elected Frank W. Johnson as their colonel, and with a force of over 100 men started marching from the Brazos River to Anahuac to release the prisoners. On their way, they captured a contingent of Mexicans and when they arrived at the fort at Anahuac, demanded the release of the Americans. Bradburn proposed a deal. If Johnson and his men would retire some miles from the fort and release the Mexicans, he would then release Travis and the others. Johnson and his men then withdrew to Turtle Bayou, about five miles from Anahuac, on the Liberty road.

Bradburn then pulled a double-cross. He not only failed to release his prisoners, but resupplied his troops with some stores from a house the Texans had occupied, and sent word to Col. Domingo de Ugartechea, commandant at San Antonio, and Col. José de la Piedras, at Nacogdoches, notifying them of the situation.

The Texans were furious at the treachery of Bradburn. Thinking it unwise to attack his fort without artillery, they sent to Velasco for two cannons, and sent messengers asking for reinforcements. The reinforcements came in to augment Johnson's forces until finally the Texans were several hundred strong.

At Velasco, at the mouth of the Brazos, a sharp battle had been fought between the forces of Capt. John Austin[3] and Colonel Ugartechea on June 25. After a bloody fight of eleven hours, in which the Mexicans suffered thirty-five dead and fifteen wounded, Ugartechea raised the white flag of surrender. The Texans had seven dead and twenty-seven wounded. Ugartechea and his men were then furnished with provisions, stripped of their munitions, and allowed to set out for Matamoros, near the eastern coast of the Gulf of Mexico and south of the Rio Grande.

Colonel Piedras, commander of the fort at Nacogdoches, was advancing to the relief of Bradburn with a strong force, including a large group of Shawnee and Cherokee Indians. Upon hearing of this, the Texans sent a committee to meet him, and laid before him their complaints against Bradburn. Piedras

listened to them courteously and released the prisoners
Bradburn was holding. In addition, he agreed to pay for the pri-
vate property Bradburn had appropriated, and very tactfully
induced the latter to ask to be relieved of his command.
Bradburn then sailed for New Orleans, and later returned to
Mexico.[4]

There were other sources of friction between the Texans
and the Mexicans. In late September 1835, Lt. Francisco
Castañeda led his troops to Gonzales, a small town seventy miles
due east of San Antonio. Some four years previously the
colonists at Gonzales had been furnished a six-pound brass cannon for their defense against the Indians. As part of a general
plan to disarm the Texans, Castañeda was under instructions to
take back this cannon.

When Castañeda asked the Texans to surrender the cannon
they refused to give it up, so he positioned his forces on a small
hill by the Guadalupe River and waited. By October 1 he had
made no attempt to attack. The Texans, then about 150 strong,
elected John H. Moore their colonel and that night under a
cover of darkness crossed the Guadalupe and took up a position
opposite the Mexicans. Filling their cannon with scrap iron, they
painted "Come and Take It" on the cannon in large letters, and
placed it in full view of the enemy.

At dawn Colonel Moore sent a messenger asking Castañeda
to surrender. When he refused, Moore ordered his Texans to fire
the cannon and advance, whereupon the Mexicans panicked in
a complete route and ran back toward San Antonio to join the
main body of their troops. The Texans suffered no losses and
collected whatever booty the enemy left behind. It was October
2, 1835, and the Texas War for Independence against Mexico
had begun.

On October 6 the Committee of Safety for the municipality
of Nacogdoches, meeting in San Augustine, appointed Sam
Houston general and commander-in-chief of the forces of the
Nacogdoches Department. Houston was granted full powers to
raise troops, organize the forces, and do all other things per-
taining to that office.

Convinced by now that a general war was inevitable,
Houston wrote his friend Isaac Parker, offering liberal bounties

of land to volunteers from the United States if they would join the Texans in their fight against Santa Anna. He urged each man to come soon and bring a good rifle and one hundred rounds of ammunition. "Our war cry is 'liberty or death,' and our principles are to support the constitution, *and down with the Usurper!*"[5]

The letter to Parker was given wide circulation in the United States, as was the news that Gen. Martín Perfecto de Cós, brother-in-law of Santa Anna, had been appointed military governor of San Antonio de Bexar and was marching there at the head of 400 men to confiscate the property of the rebellious citizens. Mass meetings, speeches, and public subscriptions were held. When Adolphus Sterne, a prominent businessman of Nacogdoches, offered to buy rifles for the first fifty recruits, the New Orleans "Greys" (so nicknamed because of their gray uniforms) were formed and claimed the rifles. Men formed in Georgia, Alabama, Mississippi, Kentucky, Tennessee, Cincinnati, and New York.

After the imbroglio at Gonzales, volunteers flocked to the army. The "Western Army" of the colonists was organized at headquarters on the right bank of the Guadalupe, and elected Stephen Fuller Austin their commander-in-chief, with the intention to march to San Antonio and attack the place with the six-pounder they had retained. Austin accepted the command and went off to join his troops. Feeling the necessity for additional strength, he wrote to the Committee of Safety at San Felipe begging them to urge the Eastern Volunteers "to hurry on by forced marches to join him, and not to stay for cannon, or for anything."

San Antonio and Goliad were the two most militarily strategic points in all Texas—the "Keys to Texas."[6] Copano Bay, some thirty-odd miles southeast of Goliad, was the interior landing port of Aransas Bay. Consequently, it was the principal port for supplies from Mexico destined for Goliad and San Antonio. Apparently, James Fannin was one of the first to have broached the idea of a surprise attack on Goliad. The capture of the garrison at La Bahía, as the fort at Goliad was known, would cut the line of communications between San Antonio and Copano, and help prevent any Mexican troops from joining the main

Mexican army at San Antonio. In a letter dated September 18, 1835, the expedition was proposed by Fannin as follows:

> It is proposed to organize and collect the people of Cana [sic] and Bay Prairie and rendesvous at Robertson Ferry on Colorado River, on Monday 28 Inst. and proceed from thence to James Carr's [Kerr] residence on the Lavaca when proper information will be recd to guide our future operations. . . .
> Dispatch confidential messengers to Velasco, Columbia, Col Halls neighborhood and San Felippi [sic.] the last named can join the party at Carrs [James Kerr]. . . . I will attend personally to Mercers and Menefee's settlement will also turn out and should not be neglected. I will personally attend to Matagorda and Bay Prairie and will see that suitable spies and scouts are sent ahead to afford us information upon which we can rely. . . .[7]

Other than this recommendation, Fannin appears to have had no personal connection with the expedition, and some weeks later joined Austin and his troops at San Antonio, where General Cós was now headquartered.

The plan was approved and a body of men, mostly from the Matagorda area, met. A company of about fifty men was organized and elected George Morse Collinsworth, a planter, as their captain. On the night of October 6, 1835, Collinsworth and his men started marching toward Goliad when suddenly they were joined by Benjamin R. Milam. Milam was a colorful bachelor originally from Kentucky. He had been a member of the unsuccessful Long Expedition some years previously, and had been in Texas for a number of years. Like so many other Texans, he had run afoul of the Mexican authorities and found himself in prison. By the use of his wits and the greasing of a few palms he had managed to escape, and was napping under a mesquite tree when encountered by the Collinsworth forces.

Collinsworth and his group reached the garrison at La Bahía shortly before eleven o'clock on the night of October 9, and found the presidio guarded by one lonely sentinel. The Texans made a surprise attack and the sentinel managed to fire his rifle once before he was shot down. After gaining entry to the fort, the colonists then attacked the quarters of Lieutenant Colonel Sandoval, the commandant, and, after breaking his door down with an axe, took him and his fellow officers prisoner. The whole affair had taken only thirty minutes, and in the confusion some seventeen or eighteen Mexicans managed to escape. The defenders reported three privates killed and seven wounded, and twenty-one made prisoner. None of the Texans were killed, but Sam McCullough, a free black, was slightly wounded in the shoulder. For their efforts, the Texans acquired military stores to the value of $10,000 as well as some pieces of badly needed artillery, and some antiquated and out-of-date muskets, many of which were repaired and salvaged.

Shortly after midnight the first contingent of seventeen Refugio volunteers, under Capt. Ira J. Westover, arrived at Goliad. Later in the day of the tenth a second contingent from Refugio arrived, and within a few days twenty-five Irish colonists from that area arrived.

In the latter part of October, Collinsworth went to Matagorda to recruit additional men for La Bahía, and then with a group of men, including Ben Milam, headed for San Antonio to join Austin. As he had received orders from Austin that the fort of La Bahía be retained, he left the presidio under the command of Capt. Philip Dimitt, a strict disciplinarian who had as his motto "lack of discipline brings confusion, and confusion brings defeat."[8]

Lipantitlán was a tiny Mexican fort on the west bank of the Nueces River, not too far from San Patricio, some fifty miles southwest of Goliad. A way station and a custom inspection point for land-borne traffic between East Texas and the interior of Mexico, the garrison was supposed to harbor a number of Texas prisoners of war. Dimitt sent his adjutant, Ira J. Westover, and some forty men to capture the fort and release the prisoners.

Westover and his men proceeded to Refugio and picked up a few volunteers for their party. Receiving information from a friendly Mexican that the commandant of Lipantitlán, with eighty-five troops, was on the Goliad road waiting to intercept him, Westover and his men flanked the enemy captain and took the garrison and liberated several prisoners of war with no difficulty. According to John J. Linn, *alcalde* of Victoria, who was among Westover's party, the "garrison" consisted of several Mexican soldiers and "the fort was a simple embankment of earth, lined within by fence rails to hold the dirt in place, and would have answered tolerably well, perhaps, for a second-rate hog pen."[9] The captured munitions of war consisted of two four-pounder cannon, eight *escopetas*, or old Spanish guns, and three or four pounds of powder, but no balls for the guns were discovered.

At the Presidio La Bahía, on December 20, 1835, Captain Dimitt and his company of volunteers, most of whom were from the South Texas area, drew up a Declaration of Independence of Texas from Mexico. It declared that

> the former province and Department of Texas is, and of a right out to be, a free sovereign and independent State: That we hereto set our names, pledge to each other our lives, our fortunes and our sacred honor to sustain this dec-laration—relying with entire confidence upon the co-oper-ation of our fellow-citizens on the approving smiles of the God of the living to aid and conduct us victoriously through the struggle, to the enjoyment of peace, union and good government; and invoking His maledictions if we should either equivocate or, in any manner whatever, prove our-selves unworthy of the high destiny at which we aim.

There were ninety-two signers to the document, and about one-third redeemed their pledges with their lives, most of them as members of Fannin's command.

A flag of independence was then made and run up. The flag was of white cotton two yards long and a yard wide, and in the center was a bloody severed arm holding a crimson sword against a white background. The arm was interpreted as a sym-bol of strength, suggesting that Texans would rather cut off their arms than remain a part of Mexico.

A committee of six men then rode to the Provisional Government that had recently been formed at San Felipe and presented the declaration. Nothing was done, as a majority of the delegates present, and the General Council, still wanted to remain under Mexico as per the Constitution of 1824.

2

A PROVISIONAL GOVERNMENT IS FORMED

A Consultation had been scheduled to assemble October 15, 1835, to discuss the future of Texas, but on the appointed date there weren't enough delegates present to make a quorum. The Consultation was postponed until November 1, to meet at San Felipe de Austin, and leave was granted for those desiring to join Austin's army at San Antonio. Sam Houston, a delegate from Nacogdoches, arrived in late October to find that Austin was with his troops at Salado Creek, about five miles east of San Antonio, and many members of the Consultation were with him. Houston decided he would ride to see Austin and bring back enough delegates so that the Consultation could get down to business.

Upon arriving at the campsite he met a dispirited Austin, whose army was completely disorganized, undrilled, and without discipline. As volunteers with no regular enlistment or oath, they would come and go at will and sometimes left in squads to go home. Austin later wrote the president of the Consultation that his army was nothing but an undisciplined militia, and of very poor quality. It was his opinion that the officers, from himself on down, were inexperienced in military service and that with such a force San Antonio could not be successfully attacked. In his discouragement, Austin offered the command of the army to Houston, who declined in the interests of harmony.

Austin recognized the necessity of organizing a provisional

9

government and providing means for its support. Austin and Houston addressed the troops, informing them of the necessity of enough delegates to leave the army and return to San Felipe. After a discussion among themselves, the army voted to send all delegates in their ranks to San Felipe for the Consultation beginning November 1. Houston and the delegates then returned to San Felipe, while Austin stayed with the troops.

Among the volunteers who joined Austin was sandy-haired James Bowie, who had come galloping into camp on a small gray mare with six volunteers from Louisiana. His famous knife was secured in his sash, and a rifle slung from his saddle.[1] Like Milam, Bowie had been a member of the ill-fated Long Expedition some years previously and he had prospered since deciding to make Texas his permanent home. He had joined the Roman Catholic church and in 1830 had taken as his bride none other than the beautiful Ursula Veramendi, daughter of Don Juan Martín de Veramendi, vice-governor and later governor of the state of Coahuila-Texas. In addition to two children and a fine home near Saltillo in the Coahuila section of the dual state, he was the possessor of nearly three-quarters of a million acres of land. In September 1833, he had lost his wife, his two children, and his parents-in-law in a vast cholera epidemic that also took the life of Stephen Austin's brother.[2]

Austin sent Bowie and Capt. James W. Fannin, Jr., together with ninety men—many of whom were boys of fourteen to twenty—on a mission of scouting and obtaining badly needed supplies for the troops. In addition, they were to select a better campsite for the army near San Antonio. Santa Anna's brother-in-law, Gen. Martín Perfecto de Cós, had entered San Antonio on October 7. He was strongly fortified and equipped with heavy artillery, cavalry, muskets, bayonets, and lances, and Austin estimated Cós' strength at 700 men compared to his own 400.

Fannin and Bowie spent several days in their reconnoitering of the general area, and Cós was quickly informed of their activities by many of San Antonio's Mexican residents. The two finally selected a position within a mile and a half of the town, in the bend of the San Antonio River, and some 500 yards from the old mission of Nuestra Señora de la Purísima Concepción de

Acuña, commonly referred to as the Mission Concepción. Rather than take their weary troops and horses back to join Austin and his army, the two commanders picked a good defensive position and decided to camp there for the night.

A level plain in the bend of the river was bordered by heavily wooded land, to form two nearly equal sides of a broad wedge. The area provided a natural fortification against any artillery fire. A steep decline dropped some six to ten feet to the river bottom, so that the river itself protected the rear. The strategy was for the men to dig steps in the bluff, and if an attack came half of the men would go up the steps and fire, then drop back to reload while the other half replaced them and continued the fire. With Fannin's Brazos Guards on one side of the bend and Bowie's Los Leoncitos on the other, it was virtually impossible for an attacking force to form an effective frontal charge. At the same time it was difficult for any cavalry to encircle the defenders because of the river. Sentries were then posted for the night.

The morning of October 28 saw Cós approaching in the fog with his force of about 300 infantry, 100 cavalry, and two small cannons. The fog began lifting around eight o'clock and the Mexican infantry advanced to about 200 yards on the Texans' right. When the infantry opened fire it was ineffective due to the excellent defensive position of the colonists. After about ten minutes Cós moved one of his six-pounders up to fire at a range of eighty yards, but it, too, proved ineffective. When the Mexican cannoneers would stop to reload, the Texans would move up the bluff and pick them off. Finally, after several ineffective charges by the infantry and cavalry, and his artillery having absolutely no effect, Cós retreated with his demoralized troops. The Texans had won the Battle of Concepción. The Texans had one man killed and none wounded, while the Mexicans lost nearly 100 men killed and wounded, including some officers.

Operations at San Antonio then ground to a halt. At a council of war on November 2, Austin asked his officers for their opinion as to the advisability of a direct assault upon the heavily fortified Mexican positions. It was pointed out the Texans had no heavy artillery to support any attack. When Austin called for a vote, Fannin, Bowie, Milam, Edward Burleson, and all other officers present (with one exception) voted against an attack. The Texans then laid siege to Cós and his army.

On November 3, 1835, a quorum of fifty-five members representing the thirteen municipalites of Texas met in San Felipe de Austin in a little frame building of one floor. Among its most important work was the adoption of a plan for a provisional government and for the formation of a regular army. The government was to consist of a governor, a lieutenant governor, and a general council, composed of one member from each municipality of Texas. The military plan contemplated two things — the creation of a regular army and the organization of the militia.[3]

In the election for governor, Henry Smith, a hot-tempered man from Brazoria, was elected by nine votes over Stephen F. Austin. James W. Robinson, a member of the Peace Party from Nacogdoches, was elected lieutenant governor. Unfortunately, the General Council was set up with ill-defined and almost co-ordinate powers with the governor. In a letter to the Consultation, Austin requested he be relieved from command of the army. His request was granted and he, William H. Wharton, and Dr. Branch T. Archer were commissioned to go to the United States to enlist aid and sympathy for the Texas cause and to borrow one million dollars.

The army was to consist of 1,120 men—including both officers and enlisted men—and be composed of regulars and volunteers. The regulars were to be enlisted for two years and the volunteers, called "permanent volunteers," were enlisted for, and during the continuance of, the war. Officers and privates were to receive the same pay as those in the regular army of the United States, and each private and noncommissioned officer was promised a bounty of 640 acres of land. Later, as an incentive to enlist in the regular army rather than with the volunteers, an additional bounty of 160 acres of land and $24 was offered the regulars; one-half of the money was to be paid when the recruit reported at headquarters, and the balance on the first quarterly payday thereafter. In addition, there was a corps of Rangers, commanded by a major, and subject to the commander-in-chief when in the field. The rangers' term of service was fixed at one year, and their pay was $1.25 per day. In addition, they were to furnish their own rations, horses, and equipment.[4]

For militia duty, all able-bodied men between the ages of sixteen and fifty were declared qualified. The municipality was to be the basis of organization, and companies comprising fifty-six men were to elect their officers—a captain and a first and second lieutenant. If there were three companies in a municipality, a major would be elected to command the entire force. Four companies were entitled to a lieutenant colonel; five companies would comprise a regiment and be entitled to a colonel; and more than five companies would call for a brigadier general.

The commander-in-chief was appointed by the Consultation and commissioned by the governor, and was subject to the orders of both the governor and the General Council. He had the rank of major-general, and was to be "commander-in-chief of all the forces called into public service during the war."

Sam Houston, at the age of forty-one, was appointed major-general and commander-in-chief. On November 14, 1835, the Consultation adjourned, to be succeeded the next day by the provisional government that it had created. It was agreed that the delegates would assemble in convention March 1 at Washington-on-the-Brazos.

Houston was an excellent choice for the position of commander of all Texas forces. A natural born leader with a charismatic personality, he was a powerful physical specimen. He was six feet three inches in height with a reputed forty-eight-inch chest. Born in the Tidewater section of Virginia, in his youth he had migrated to Tennessee with his widowed mother and nine brothers and sisters. In 1813, shortly after his twentieth birthday, he had joined the regular army of the United States as a private, and due to his leadership qualities had been quickly promoted to second lieutenant. He had been a member of the infantry in Andrew Jackson's army in the latter's campaign against the Creek Indians, and had been severely wounded twice in the Battle of Horseshoe Bend. By distinguishing himself in the battle, he had been given a battlefield promotion to first lieutenant by Jackson.

After the war, Houston had stayed in the regular army for five years before resigning his commission. He returned home to Marysville and became a lawyer. Successful in his practice, and popular, he was elected congressman from the Nashville district in Tennessee; was elected major-general of militia; and was later elected governor of the state. As he was beginning his campaign for a second term his marriage broke up, and the unhappy Houston resigned his office. After a three-year detour to reside in the Cherokee Nation West, now Oklahoma, he crossed the Red River to settle in eastern Texas in Nacogdoches. There he quickly established a successful law practice and became a leader in the community and in affairs affecting Texas.

This, then, was the man the Texans chose to lead them into battle.

The new commander-in-chief set up headquarters in the front room of the Virginia House in San Felipe de Austin, and quickly discovered that he had a title but little real authority. From the beginning there was conflict between the governor and the General Council, with dissension, intrigue, backbiting, confusion, and inefficiency among the various factions. Houston was of the opinion the first thing the army should do was to appoint capable regular officers, as the rank and file would then enlist to serve under capable leaders. But he himself didn't have the authority to appoint them. That appointment power rested in the hands of the General Council. Even as commander-in-chief, the only officers Houston was allowed to appoint were those on his personal staff of one adjutant general, one inspector general, one quartermaster, a surgeon general, and four aides-de-camp. The Military Affairs Committee of the Provisional Government was dragging its feet not only in providing officers, but also in authorizing money for the recruitment of soldiers.

In his disgust, Houston later wrote that "All new States are infested, more or less, by a class of noisy, second rate men, who are always in favor of rash and extreme measures. But Texas was absolutely overrun by such men."[5]

In an endeavor to man his army with officers, on November 13 Houston wrote a confidential letter to James Fannin, serving as a captain with the volunteer army at San Antonio, and offered him an appointment as inspector general in the regular army with the rank of colonel. Houston was of the opinion it would be unwise to try to dislodge General Cós from his well-entrenched fortifications at San Antonio. It was his opinion that the Texans should never have passed the Guadalupe "without the proper munitions of war to reduce San Antonio."[6] He suggested to Fannin it would be better to fall back to Goliad and Gonzales, and furlough most of his army until they had sufficient heavy artillery.

James Walker Fannin, Jr., was from Columbus, Georgia, and had moved to Texas in the fall of 1834 with his wife, Minerva, and their two daughters. Born about January 1, 1805, it was said that he was the illegitimate son of a Georgia planter, a Dr. Isham Fannin. He was adopted and reared by his paternal grandfather, James W. Walker, on a plantation near Marion, Georgia. On July 1, 1819, at the age of fourteen years and six months, Fannin was admitted to the United States Military Academy at West Point under the name of James F. Walker. He remained at that institution as a cadet until November 1821. In that month he had a quarrel with a fellow student which ended in a fist fight, according to his cousin Martha, and left the school. Some reports say he ran away, while others say he resigned. During his more than two years at the academy, although he was ranked sixteenth in a class of eighty-six, he remained in the fourth, or plebe, class, when he left the school.

Like a number of men who came to Texas to enroll in the cause, Fannin had dubious credentials. For years he carried on a correspondence with his half-sister Eliza, who was about eleven years his junior. He wrote her enthusiastic letters telling her of his trips to Cuba to purchase sugar and in one letter told her about his purchase of "two parrots, two guinea pigs and various other odd creatures, including two blue-headed, ring striped pigeons" that he was purchasing for her. For himself, he was keeping "the finest collection of shells you have ever seen — nay, ever read about."

Fannin might have been purchasing sugar in Cuba, but at the same time he was engaged in the illegal slave trade, smuggling slaves from Africa and Spanish Cuba into the United States. For some of these ventures he had partners, and he either overextended himself or was a poor businessman, because he was frequently in debt and had to stall his creditors. He had unpaid notes dating back as far as 1828, and at least once was arrested for nonpayment of debt and issuing drafts that were not honored for payment.

When Fannin came to Texas he operated a sugar plantation on the San Bernard River, but his main occupation was smuggling slaves. In September 1835 he wrote one of his creditors, a Mr. Thompson: "I have since made a good trip, having brought for myself and others 152 negroes in May last (1835), but can not realize any cash for them until March or April, when you shall be fully paid every cent I owe you. . . . I am settled on Caney Creek, midway between Brazoria and Matagorda."[7]

As late as January 12, 1836, just before Fannin went down the coast to Copano and Goliad, he entered into an ambitious contract with Joseph Mims of Brazoria. Mims owned 3,000 acres of land on the San Bernard. The two men entered into a farming partnership valued at $50,000. For his half, Mims put in a number of slaves, cattle, oxen, mules, horses, carts, hogs, plows, and other farm equipment. Fannin put in a number of slaves valued at $17,250 and signed notes for the remaining $7,750 to be paid in five equal installments.

Once Fannin arrived in Texas, it didn't take him long to involve himself in affairs between the Mexican government and the colonists. During the winter of 1834-1835, he visited Maj. Francis S. Belton, who commanded the post at Fort Mobile, Mobile Point, Alabama, and stated that Texas would need aid from friends in the United States, particularly from a few experienced officers. Then, on August 27, 1835, he wrote the major "when the hurly is begun, we will be glad to see as many West Point boys as can be spared — many of whom are known to me." Fannin predicted that the Consultation, to be held October 15, 1835, would declare Texas independent, and he asked the major for permission to present his name to the Consultation as an officer qualified and willing to command the Texas army. Belton replied to the letter, but neither declined nor agreed to permit use of his name, so Fannin recommended to the president of the Consultation that Belton be offered an appointment in the proposed Texas military organization. He also proposed to

Governor Henry Smith that the army be organized largely under the command of West Point officers.

When Stephen F. Austin was guest of honor at the banquet given at Brazoria on September 8, 1835, Fannin was in attendance and responded to the wordy toast: "Union. May the people of Texas unite roses, white and red, and their only emulation shall be who will do the most for the public good." He later pledged $500 toward the purchase of arms and munitions of war, and also raised and trained a company of soldiers, the "Brazos Guards," and as their captain participated with them in the Battle of Gonzales on October 2. Later that day, he addressed a letter to his fellow citizens urging them to "come to Gonzales armed and equipped for war, even to the knife."

After the affair at Gonzales, Fannin was a member of a committee that, on October 6, sent a message to Austin requesting he come to Gonzales and bring all the aid possible. Then, when Austin accepted the command of the volunteers at San Antonio, Fannin and his Brazos Guards went there to serve under him.

3

DREAMS OF GLORY

On November 10, Fannin and 150 men had been ordered by Austin to intercept a Mexican convoy reported to be bringing supplies to Cós' army at San Antonio. Fannin went as far as the Rio Frio on the Laredo road searching for the convoy. When he was not joined by a supporting force, as had been planned, he decided to return to the main camp. On November 18 he wrote Houston:

> With regard to falling back. . . . I must admit it to be a safest course. On the other hand, I am fully convinced that with 250 men, well chosen & properly drilled . . . that the place can be taken by storm.[1]

A few hours later he again wrote Houston:

> . . . with regard to my acceptance, I would prefer a command in the line, if I could be actively Engaged. Having elected one Maj Genl—Will they not also make two Brig Genls? If so, would not my claims be equal to any other? If I can get either—I would prefer it—and I respectfully request your influence for one — Otherwise I will accept of the appointment you tender me. . . . But I am well satisfied, that I can fill either of the posts, *better than any officer, who has yet been in Command.* . . .[2]

18

Four days later, on November 22, Fannin requested to be discharged from the army on "the absolute necessity of returning home," and was granted an honorable discharge. Austin, who considered him to be very efficient, recommended him for an appointment as an officer in the future regular army of Texas.

Fannin, whose two years as a military cadet at West Point had apparently given him an exalted idea as to his military capabilities, quickly followed his letter to Houston's headquarters. In an interview with his superior, he protested that the position as inspector-general offered him was not suitable for his experience and ability. Houston refused his demand to be made a brigadier general, but said he would ask the council to appoint him a colonel. Fannin then wrote Governor Smith his views on the size of the army, and on December 4 the letter was referred to the Military Affairs Committee. Fannin held the view the size of the army should be doubled. "If an army be at all requisite," he said, "it sh'd *be large enough to answer the [purpose] of its creation* . . . .The case appears to me so plain that I can not doubt but you will see it in the same light. With this conviction, I will proceed to the main subject — By virtue of your delegated powers & exigency of the case increase the 'Regular Army' to another Brigade of like numbers with the one already ordered."[3]

Inasmuch as a brigade calls for the rank of brigadier general, Fannin's letter might have been a ploy for him to secure that rank. If so, it didn't work, but on December 7 the council offered him a commission as colonel of artillery in the regular army and he accepted. The military committee thought highly of his idea to increase the size of the forces, and authorized Houston to try to recruit 5,000 auxiliary volunteers. William Barret Travis was offered a commission as major of artillery in the regular army, turned it down, and then accepted a commission as lieutenant colonel of the cavalry.

On December 20, 1835, Fannin was sworn in as colonel in the regular army. Having so ardently sung his own praises to Houston in requesting he be made a brigadier general, he then showed the stuff of which he was made. Houston, in his capacity as commander-in-chief, sent him written orders to open a recruiting station at Matagorda, on the eastern coast, and to acknowledge receipt of the order in writing. Fannin did neither.

When the general then sent him orders to report to headquarters, he ignored them and went to Velasco instead.

With the departure of Austin to the United States as commissioner, the 400 men at San Antonio elected Edward Burleson, a noted Indian fighter, as their colonel and commander, and there was discussion as to whether to continue the siege or retire to Goliad. The siege had reached a stalemate and the winter season with its biting northers was at hand. The volunteer army was short on clothing for the winter, provisions, and forage, and they still had no heavy artillery to use against the fortress of the Alamo with its battery of twenty-one pieces of heavy artillery. In addition, they were about half the strength of Cós and his army, and they knew the Mexican commander had requested reinforcements from Mexico. In addition, there were rumors that Santa Anna would soon be marching into Texas with an army of 10,000.[4]

Goliad was the perfect place for the army to move to if they lifted the siege of San Antonio. There Texas troops could cut off the enemy's communication with the seaboard and keep the frontier under observation. In addition, it was an excellent point from which to march in the event of hostile movements being made by Santa Anna's troops upon Texas frontier settlements. Burleson sent James Bowie to Goliad to investigate the situation there.

By December 3 the army had about decided to lift the siege and move to Goliad when the situation suddenly changed. The next day the Texans received information from Lt. Jesús "Comanche" Cuellar, a Mexican officer who had deserted from Cós' army, that the strength of the Mexican defenders was overestimated, their camp disorganized, and their morale poor.[5]

After much quizzing of Cuellar, it was decided he was telling the truth and that an attack upon the town and the Alamo was feasible. Burleson gave his assent to the venture and decided to stay at headquarters with a reserve force. Then the grizzled veteran, Ben Milam, stepped in front of headquarters and cried, "Who will follow old Ben Milam into San Antonio?" Three hundred volunteers stepped forward. The hour for the attack was set at just before daylight of the morning of December 5.

The attacking forces were divided into two columns. The

first was commanded by Milam. The New Orleans Greys had recently arrived from Louisiana, and Maj. Robert C. Morris of the Greys was appointed his second-in-command. The second column was to be headed by Col. Frank Johnson. The plan called for the two columns to attack the town proper, while Lt. Col. James C. Neill, a regular in the artillery, would make a side maneuver on the heavily defended Alamo.

At the appointed hour the assault began. The battle was a grueling one, with the Texans literally going from house to house as troops did in World War II, tunneling themselves inside with the use of crowbars to cut holes through the roofs or walls. On the third day the gallant Milam was killed when struck in the head by a bullet as he entered the courtyard of Vice-governor Veramendi, father-in-law of James Bowie, near the plaza.

On December 9, Cós, although receiving some 600 reinforcements the night before, asked for terms of capitulation while the battle for the plaza still raged. The articles of surrender were signed on the eleventh and Cós, giving his parole to leave Texas and not return, departed for Mexico and took his 1,100 troops with him. During the battle twelve Texans were killed and eighteen wounded. It was estimated the Mexicans suffered 150 killed and an untold number wounded.

With the departure of Cós and his beaten army, not a Mexican soldier was in Texas north of the Rio Grande. A wave of rejoicing swept the colonists, and many people thought the war was over. The army at San Antonio quickly shrunk as many of the Texan volunteers went back to their farms, ranches and businesses, and the commander, Burleson, resigned his commission and went home to his family. Command of the force then passed to Colonel Johnson, who promptly styled himself "Commander-in-Chief of the Volunteers," and sent a letter to the General Council, signing himself as such.[6]

Sam Houston had many headaches as commander of the small Texas army, and one of his earliest was given him by the proposed Matamoros Expedition. As early as October 15, Capt. Philip Dimitt had written a letter to Austin suggesting such an expedition to Matamoros, a town of some 12,000 inhabitants 274 miles slightly southeast of San Antonio, just south of the Rio

Grande and near the eastern coast of Mexico and the Gulf of Mexico. Some believe the idea was first broached to various Texas leaders by Capt. Pedro Julian Miracle, Santa Anna's clever spy.[7]

At first glance it seemed there may be good reasons for taking the city. It was an excellent staging area for any Mexican army to invade Texas, and its capture would help keep the war out of Texas and in Mexico. The post was yielding better than $100,000 per month in revenues and it was thought it would yield considerably more than that if properly handled. On December 2, prior to taking his troops to reinforce the army at San Antonio, Dimitt published a document reviving his idea, and James Fannin was highly in favor of such an expedition.

At first Governor Smith was in favor of the proposal, and on December 17 he ordered Houston to proceed with its organization. The same day, from his headquarters at San Felipe, Houston ordered Col. James Bowie, in whom he always had great faith, to conduct the campaign "and, if possible, reduce the place and retain possession until further orders. . . . "[8] Cognizant of the fact Cós and his army were on their way back to Mexico, he further ordered: "If any officers or men who have, at any time, been released on *parole* should he be taken in arms, they will be proper subjects for the consideration of court-martial. Great caution is necessary in the country of an enemy."[9] Houston then took a look at the map and changed his mind about the feasibility of a Matamoros Expedition. The logistical situation was terrible when he considered the inaccessibility of the place, the difficulty of supplying the garrison if it was taken, and the immense forces and supplies needed to undertake the project on account of its distance from the settled parts of Texas.

It is more than likely that by now Houston had heard of the disastrous results of the Tampico Expedition, and that helped him change his mind. On November 6, 1835, the schooner *Mary Jane* had sailed from New Orleans with 130 soldiers under the command of Mexican General José Antonio Mexia. About two-thirds of the group were Americans — including the Tampico Blues, who were on their way to join the Texan cause — and the others English, French, and a few Germans.

A couple of days out at sea General Mexia announced the

expedition was headed for Tampico and induced a large number of the troops to join him in an endeavor to take the city. Tampico was attacked on November 15, and Mexia and his army were routed. The general and his party managed to escape and get back to the Brazos, and eventually to New Orleans. Of thirty-one prisoners left behind in Tampico, three died of their wounds and the remaining twenty-eight were court-martialed and shot on December 14, 1835.

The problem of supply was an important military problem during the Texas Revolution, and Copano had become the principal port for Goliad and San Antonio. Houston, therefore, decided to concentrate his forces at and near Copano, where they could be organized, disciplined, and trained. Troops always need fresh water and to be fed, and at Copano there was plenty of fresh water and good beef to be had. In addition, controlling Copano would be denying it as a base for the enemy.

On December 30, 1835, Houston ordered Colonel Fannin to transport the volunteers at the mouth of the Brazos to Copano, by sea.[10] Then his plans ran into a snag.

After the fall of San Antonio and the departure of Burleson to his home, Frank Johnson and a Dr. James Grant had concocted their own scheme (and for their own purposes) to march upon Matamoros. A regiment consisting of four companies of infantry, one of cavalry, and one of artillery was formed and Johnson, a major of artillery in the regular army, was elected as colonel and commander of the force.

Grant, a native of Scotland who was generally described as arrogant, overbearing and ruthless, was a Mexican citizen. He had been a prosperous mine owner in the Coahuila portion of Coahuila-Texas and had owned vast estates there. A man of influence, for a time he had been a member of the legislature of the province but for some reason he had gained the enmity of Don Martín Perfecto de Cós, brother-in-law of Santa Anna. As a result of the enmity he lost not only his influence but, worse yet, his estates. Leaving Coahuila fearful for his life, he had joined the Texan cause and had fought valiantly at the battle for San Antonio, and had been wounded in the action.

The Johnson and Grant project against Matamoros had been organizing long prior to the final decision to storm San Antonio. Their intention was to create a Republic of the Rio Grande by carving from Mexican territory an independent state bounded by the Nueces River on the north and a line drawn from Tampico straight across to the Pacific, with the capital at Laredo. In the process, Dr. Grant would liberate his vast estates at Parras, deep in the interior of Mexico.

Both Dimitt and Austin, who had at first been inclined toward a march on Matamoros, changed their minds when apprised of the intentions of the duo, unless the army was led by a Mexican general with Federalist Mexican troops, as they were both sensitive to the political situation in Mexico. Smith and Houston were appalled by the idea, and Houston denounced the plan as being little short of piracy. It probably had quite a bit to do with his deciding upon Copano as a training and staging area. From a military standpoint, Houston was trying to create an army capable of meeting the *"usurper,"* as he referred to Santa Anna, in the field by March 1. He saw no reason why the army should be used to recover the confiscated estates of Dr. Grant, especially as he knew that Mexican pride would not allow the Mexicans to suffer the loss of San Antonio without an attempt at revenge. Houston fully expected the Mexican dictator to put at least 10,000 soldiers in the field when he invaded Texas.

Grant painted a rosy picture of the rich spoils to be taken from the cities of Tamaulipas, Nuevo Leon, Coahuila, and San Luis Potosí, and his proposals fell on willing ears among the volunteers and adventurers at San Antonio.[11]

On the last day of 1835, Grant, with around 400 volunteers, left San Antonio for Goliad on the first leg of his journey to Matamoros. His partner, Johnson, left for the seat of government at San Felipe to get authorization from the government for the invasion across the Rio Grande. He explained to the General Council that the army was on its way, and would be welcomed by the Mexicans below the border as deliverers from tyranny. The council approved the expedition and offered the command to Johnson; in addition, they appropriated several hundred dollars to pay for wagons and teams which Grant had impressed.

Governor Smith, who thought the proposed expedition was

madness, urged Johnson not to undertake it, and Johnson changed his mind. Then, on January 6, Fannin rode into town with news of men and munitions which were being assembled at the mouth of the Brazos for a quick dash into Mexico and offered to command the expedition.

Continuing their meddling into military affairs, the council decided to create an office known as "military agent," which would serve as field commander and be responsible not to Houston, the duly elected commander-in-chief of the forces, but to the council. Fannin was appointed "Agent for and in behalf of the Provisional Government of Texas, with power of making loans or of impressment,"[12] and accepted the office and command of the proposed venture. At the same time, the council appointed Dr. Grant as commander-in-chief of volunteers. Then, on January 7, Johnson, after discovering Fannin had accepted the appointment, changed his mind and once more the council appointed him to lead the expedition—all of this without the knowledge of Houston—and for a while the army had four commanders. When Houston heard about the situation he complained, "The army has been stolen from under me."

On January 9, Fannin published a proclamation in the *Telegraph and Texas Register*. It read:

ATTENTION, VOLUNTEERS!
To the West, face: March!
An expedition to the west has been ordered by the General Council, and the Volunteers from Bejar, Goliad, Velasco, and elsewhere, are ordered to rendezvous at San Patricio, between the 24th and 27th, inst. and report to the officer in command. The fleet convoy will sail from Velasco under my charge, on or about the 18th, and all who feel disposed to join it, and aid in keeping the war out of Texas, and at the same time cripple the enemy in their resources at home, are invited to enter the ranks forthwith. . . .

Fannin added that the volunteers would be paid out of the spoils of war taken from the enemy. Then on the tenth, Johnson issued a like proclamation, calling his the *Federal* volunteer army, marching for "the country west of the Rio Grande and under the flag of 1824."

4

ON TO MATAMOROS

Houston had been unable to find out if any troops and supplies had been arriving at Velasco, so he sent Capt. George W. Poe, his acting adjutant general, there to hand-deliver two letters he had written Fannin. One letter informed Fannin that all volunteers were ordered to Copano and to remain there until they had orders to advance; at the same time he requested Fannin, if possible, to report in person at headquarters as soon as practicable. Apparently, Fannin ignored both letters, as they were endorsed by Poe: "Left in my hands by Fannin."

To add to Houston's worries, he had received a courier from Neill, now in command of San Antonio and the Alamo, with the unwelcome news that Johnson and Grant were on their way to Matamoros, going by way of Goliad and Refugio. In their haste to leave San Antonio, they had stripped the garrison of all of its provisions, clothing, medicines, small arms and ammunition, and even blankets for the sick and wounded. In addition, the troops were complaining because they had never been paid.

At first Neill had planned to join the expedition, but had changed his mind when he realized San Antonio would be left defenseless. He had stayed behind with Capt. Juan N. Seguin's loyal Mexican *Tejanos*, the sick and wounded, and his own artillery company.

Fannin, with $5,000 he had received from the council,

returned to Velasco, where a number of volunteers from Georgia were encamped. Johnson, who had received $2,000 from Fannin, went to Goliad, where Grant had preceded him with the volunteers from San Antonio on the road to Matamoros.

Governor Smith was furious with the council for meddling in military affairs, and tried to veto the appointments given Fannin, Johnson, and Grant.

Most of the members chosen for the original General Council were men of substance and ability, but after the Provisional Government had been formed, it wasn't too long before some of the competent members resigned to accept various appointments in the government or army, and others left to return home to look after their families. Under these circumstances it wasn't too long before the council was composed of inferior personnel—some of the "noisy and second-rate men," as Houston described them.

This council promptly did as they saw fit and frequently passed laws without a quorum being present. They were jealous of Houston and his reputation, and in an effort to get him out of the way, on December 15 they ordered him to transfer his headquarters from San Felipe, where the government was, to the small hamlet of Washington-on-the-Brazos, about fifty miles away. Houston delayed for a while, but finally moved on Christmas Day.

The council overrode Smith's veto. Then, when Smith found out Johnson and Grant had denuded the garrison at San Antonio and were on their way to Matamoros, he exploded. To emphasize his anger at the council in their interference in what he thought were affairs of no concern to them, on January 10 he issued a statement calling the council "corrupt scoundrels" and denounced their acts in no uncertain terms. In addition, he demanded an apology from the council and suggested it either agree to cooperate with him or else dissolve until after March 1, 1836, when a convention of delegates was to be held at Washington-on-the-Brazos.

As an answer to the governor, the council vilified and impeached him and elevated Lieutenant Governor James Robinson to the governorship. The feisty Smith refused to give up his office, seizing the state archives and keeping the official seal.

In December, Houston had been issued orders by the council to visit the Cherokees and other tribes and negotiate a treaty of neutrality with them in the event of further hostilities. By now, Houston was in favor of complete independence from Mexico, and in the squabbles between Governor Smith and the council he remained loyal to Smith, as did Travis and Bowie, and took orders only from the governor: "I will set out in less than an hour for the Army. I will do all that I can. I am told that Frank Johnson and Fannin have obtained from the Military Committee orders to proceed and reduce Matamoros. It may not be so. There was no Quorum, and the Council could not give power. I will proceed with great haste to the Army and there I can know all."[1]

It was a cold and windy winter day when Houston left for Goliad, accompanied by his aide, Maj. George Hockley, and others of his staff. On the way they encountered an angry Capt. Philip Dimitt and his men, all on foot. On January 9, Grant, on his way to Refugio, where he expected to meet Fannin, had arrived at Goliad and not only seized three cannons which Neill had sent from the Alamo but also forced the garrison to surrender twenty of their horses—their entire complement—and each the personal property of its rider. This last was a severe blow as it deprived the people of Matagorda and Refugio their means of transportation home, as well as using the beasts for scouting and courier and foraging services.

Arriving at Goliad on the night of January 14, Houston and his staff found no Fannin, nor any supplies. Johnson was also nowhere around. Maj. Robert C. Morris, who had fought at San Antonio with the New Orleans Greys, was in command, and his Greys were eager to participate in the Matamoros adventure.

The next morning Houston made an impassioned speech to the troops still in Goliad, trying to dissuade the men from participating in the reckless venture of Johnson and Grant. While in the middle of his speech he was interrupted by a courier from San Antonio. The courier reported that two of Colonel Neill's scouts had discovered that two of Santa Anna's generals had led separate troops across the Rio Grande in an invasion of Texas, and were on their way to attack San Antonio. Houston was surprised, as he had thought it would be March before Santa Anna would be able to get an invasion under way.

When Houston finished speaking, Capt. Thomas K. Pearson of the New Orleans Greys made a speech of rebuttal. The captain pointed out that he and his men had landed at Paso Cavallo the previous November, and aided in transporting an eighteen-pound cannon from Dimitt's landing to San Antonio—a feat of engineering which caused his arrival at San Antonio to be three days after the capitulation of Cós. Subsequently, he and his men had gone to Goliad and waited and waited and had seen no action. The time of waiting was over, he insisted, and they should be on their way.

Neill was calling for help to defend the Alamo, and at the same time he asked Houston for a furlough so he could visit his sick family. Almost immediately Bowie rode into camp, asking for men to go back with him to help Neill. Explaining the situation to all the troops at Goliad, Houston called for volunteers to go back to San Antonio with Bowie. Thirty men responded. He then sent Bowie and his thirty men back to Neill, with a letter granting his request for a furlough. Houston ordered him to remove all artillery from the Alamo and blow it up, as it would be impossible to hold the town with the force there.[2] Inasmuch as Neill was on the scene and knew the situation better than anyone, the general gave him some leeway to use his own judgment. Having great faith in Bowie as a capable officer, and trusting his judgment also, he left to Bowie the decision as to whether to abandon the Alamo or not.

Houston then wrote Governor Smith on January 17, enclosing Neill's letter, stating that Bowie would leave shortly for San Antonio and that within a few hours he himself, with around 200 men, would take up the march to Refugio, where he would await orders from Smith. "I do not believe that an army of such small force should advance upon Matamoros, with a hope or belief that the Mexicans will co-operate with us," he wrote. "I have no confidence in them. The disaster of Tampico should teach us a lesson to be noted in our future operations. . . . I would myself have marched to Bexar, but the 'Matamoros fever' rages so high, that I must see Colonel Ward's men."[3]

William Ward was the commander of a well-equipped battalion recently arrived from Georgia, and Houston had entrusted it and its supplies to Fannin.

When Neill wrote Houston complaining of Johnson and Grant stripping the garrison at San Antonio, he had also written Governor Smith the facts and asked for a furlough. Smith also granted his request, and ordered William Barret Travis, then on recruiting duty at San Felipe (Austin), to proceed to the Alamo and relieve Neill. Travis immediately left for the Alamo and took thirty men with him.

When Major Morris, Captain Pearson, and their troops departed for Refugio to meet with Dr. Grant, Houston and his staff rode along with them. When they reached Refugio, once more they found no Fannin, no Ward, and no supplies — contrary to Houston's orders of December 30 and January 6. On the night of January 20 the intriguing Colonel Johnson galloped in and presented Houston with a set of orders from the General Council, relieving Houston as commander-in-chief of all volunteer forces. He also gave Houston the news that Fannin and himself had been appointed military agents, subject only to the orders of the council itself, and had been given joint command of all volunteers and were instructed to proceed with the expedition to Matamoros.

Houston addressed the troops, outlining what had happened. His commission from the governor, he explained, gave him command of all the troops — regulars, militia, and volunteers. He was of the opinion the council did not have authority to countermand those orders, and he himself intended to recognize the authority of the governor. As for the troops, they would have to decide whose authority they would accept.

After mulling this over, some 200 decided against continuing to Matamoros and left for home. Two companies of the Greys crossed the river and made camp close to a Mexican plantation two miles from Refugio, to await the arrival of Fannin. The rest, including Morris and Pearson, followed Johnson and Grant.

While at Refugio, Houston wanted to send a small company of regulars, over whom his authority was not disputed, back to

Goliad to keep up a force at that place. The soldiers objected to going, saying they had been many months in the service, had not received a single cent of pay, had no shoes to wear, and were without soap to wash their clothes. Upon hearing this Houston reached into his purse and divided what money he had among the soldiers. It amounted to about five dollars for each man, and he refused to take any voucher for the same.[4]

Houston and his aides then rode back to San Felipe, where he presented himself to Governor Smith, who, in his dispute with the council, was still refusing to relinquish his position as governor.

Thoroughly disgusted with the action of the council, Houston asked for a furlough until March 1, the date the coming convention was due to assemble. His request was granted, and he went home to Nacogdoches and sought selection as a delegate to the convention. Defeated by Nacogdoches voters, he was then elected as a delegate from Refugio. He subsequently took John Forbes and his aide Hockley with him and went to Peachtree Village, near Nacogdoches in present-day Tyler County, the headquarters of the Cherokees, to negotiate a treaty of neutrality with them and other Indian tribes.

5

Santa Anna Marches

Houston's prediction that Mexican pride would cause Santa Anna to seek revenge for the defeat of Cós was proving justified. After retreating from San Antonio, Santa Anna's brother-in-law had led his army to Laredo, a small city on the Texas side of the Rio Grande, and about 150 miles slightly southwest of San Antonio.

On December 7, 1835, Santa Anna had forwarded orders to Brig. Gen. Joaquín Ramírez y Sesma, and one paragraph of those orders made it clear that foreigners waging war against Mexico were in violation of the law and were to be given no clemency. The troops should be advised of this and that as these "foreigners" had declared an annihilative war against Mexico, they should be treated in kind. On December 30 Minister of War José María Tornel signed the decree, which extended the order and made it a matter of national policy:

1. All foreigners who may land in any port of the republic or who enter it armed and for the purpose of attacking our territory shall be treated and punished as pirates, since they are not subjects of any nation at war with the republic, nor do they militate under any recognized flag.
2. Foreigners who introduce arms and munitions by land or by sea at any point of the territory now in rebellion against the government of the nation for the purpose of placing such

32

supplies in the hands of its enemies shall be treated and punished likewise.[1]

Santa Anna, headquartered at San Luis Potosí, deeply within the interior of Mexico and directly west of Tampico on the coast of the Gulf of Mexico, issued a general order of the day on December 18, 1835, which divided his army into two divisions. The First Division was placed under command of Sesma, while the Second Division, consisting of 1,800 men and six guns, had Brig. Gen. Eugenio Tolsa in command. In addition, there were Brig. Gen. Antonio Gaono, a sullen man, irritable and haughty, with 1,600 men and six guns; Brig. Gen. Juan José Andrade, with a 437-man cavalry brigade, and Brig. Gen. José Urrea, with his 300 men and 301 lances. Second in command to His Excellency *el presidente* was Maj. Gen. Vicente Filisola, an Italian who had fought in Europe under Napoleon and who had been in Mexico for some time and was now a Mexican citizen.

As early as November 17, Sesma and his forces had left San Luis Potosí with 1,000 infantry and 500 cavalry to reinforce Cós at San Antonio. For some reason dragging his feet, it took him until December 26 to reach Laredo and join up with the defeated Cós. The next day, he was followed by Filisola. Sesma and his army headed toward the small town of Guerrero a few miles southeast of Eagle Pass on the Rio Grande, while Cós and Filisola marched a few miles southwest toward Monclova, in Coahuila.

Santa Anna, the self-styled "Napoleon of the West," had troops at Guerrero, as well as in the interior of Mexico at Monclova and Saltillo. It had been his intention to launch his attack upon Texas from Laredo and Guerrero. When he heard that some 300 colonists were marching on Matamoros with the intention of seizing that port, he ordered General Urrea and his division to move on Matamoros, reinforce it, to destroy both Grant and Johnson, and to advance on Goliad and take the fort.

At Matamoros, Urrea incorporated some 300 Indians, recently recruited in Yucatan, who did not know the language and could hardly handle a rifle, into his command. He also augmented his force with some infantrymen from small groups in the garrison, a field piece, some 230 dragoons from several corps, and some companies made up of convicts.[2] When Urrea, through his intelligence, learned that Johnson and Grant had stopped at San Patricio, he was so eager to meet his enemies that he left Matamoros with just part of his cavalry, leaving the infantry and convoy behind.

Since Sam Houston had received his leave of absence from Governor Smith in late January, he had not been idle. Earlier, on January 17, he had written Smith that he had sent Col. Hugh Love to Nacogdoches to try to raise an auxiliary corps of 300 or more Indians from the Cherokee, Delaware, Shawnee, Kickapoo, and other friendly tribes. Love was authorized to offer them $7,000 in addition to one-half of all property taken by them if they agreed to serve six months.[3] Apparently Love had failed in his mission, so Houston was determined to meet with the Indians himself and try to get them to sign a treaty of neutrality.

Houston, together with his aide, Maj. George Hockley, and fellow commissioner John Forbes, arrived in Peach Tree Village[4] near Nacogdoches about the middle of February to confer with Chief Bowles of the Cherokees, and various chiefs of other tribes. After several days of dickering—together with the presentation of many gifts of knives and tomahawks to the Indians—the talks finally got under way and a treaty of neutrality was signed. There were thirteen articles in the treaty, and one of the most important specified that an area approximately fifty miles long and thirty miles wide in East Texas would be set aside for the Indians. After Texas won its independence and became an independent republic, the senate refused to ratify the treaty. Some of the land guaranteed the Indians to be theirs contained some of the finest oil wells later discovered in the United States, and to this day the Indians are suing the United States government for some of what they claim is rightfully theirs.

When James Bowie and his thirty men arrived at the Alamo pursuant to Houston's instructions, they found Neill and a force of 104 men. They had a few weapons and a few cannon but were woefully short of supplies and powder, thanks to Johnson, Grant, and their confiscation tactics. Of the men under Neill's command, only nine were born in Texas, all of them Mexicans. Among the group from many states and nations were farmers, hunter-trappers, doctors, lawyers, and other professional men.

Bowie and Neill discussed Houston's instructions to blow up

the fortifications, but inasmuch as Houston had instructed Neill to use his own judgment, Neill decided he didn't have enough oxen to move the artillery and decided against blowing up the fortress. Bowie concurred in this decision, and on February 2, 1836, wrote the governor: "The salvation of Texas depends in great measure on keeping Bexar out of the hands of the enemy. It stands on the frontier pickquet guard, and if it was in the possession of Santa Anna, there is no stronghold from which to repel him in his march to the Sabine. Colonel Neill and myself have come to the solemn resolution that we will rather die in these ditches than give them up."[5]

Travis arrived at the Alamo on February 3 with a group of men, mostly regulars, and several days later Neill left on the furlough he had been granted. Then, a day or so after Travis arrived, Davy Crockett, a noted bear hunter who had served in Congress from Tennessee along with Houston, showed up with twelve Tennesseans.

William Barret Travis was born in South Carolina and had a good education. A schoolteacher before the age of twenty, he studied law and became a successful lawyer in Claiborne, Alabama. In October 1828 he married, but the marriage proved unsuccessful. He later left his wife and baby son for Texas to become one of those many lawyers—such as Thomas J. Rusk and Houston—who fought in the Texas cause.

Travis arrived in Texas sometime around April or May of 1831, and a few months later his wife Rosanna, now with their second child, came to Texas and sought a reconciliation. Her efforts failed and she returned home and divorced Travis.

Settling in Anahuac, Travis established a successful law practice while quickly involving himself in the leading political and social circles. Eventually he moved to the center of the Anglo-American colony, San Felipe de Austin, where he opened a law office and was appointed secretary of the *ayuntamiento* in 1834.[6]

Disliking Mexicans, Travis soon became a member of the War Party seeking independence. Impetuous and arrogant, he was one of the group involved in marching on Anahuac and disarming the Mexican garrison. When the Provisional Government was formed, he quickly managed to secure a commission as a regular officer, and remained loyal to Governor Smith in his disputes with the General Council.

From the first there was conflict between Bowie and Travis, as about all the two had in common was that they were both six feet tall, of good physique, and were red-haired. Travis, who had been promoted to lieutenant colonel of cavalry in the regular army, thought he should have the command inasmuch as he had been sent by the governor. Bowie was a natural-born leader and as a colonel, although in the Rangers, outranked Travis. He was the best known fighting man in Texas except for Houston, and at age forty did not fancy submitting to the orders of a man fourteen years his junior. The men held an election and the popular Bowie was easily elected as their colonel over the cold Travis.

There was still resentment on both sides until finally, in the interest of harmony, the two soldiers arranged a truce and on February 14 wrote the governor a letter concerning the situation and the way they resolved it. The solution was to have a divided command. Bowie would command the volunteers in the garrison, and Travis was to have command of the regulars and the volunteer cavalry. Until Colonel Neill returned from his furlough, all general orders and correspondence would henceforth be signed by both men.

In any case, the quarrel became moot when, on or about February 21, Bowie developed an illness described as possibly pneumonia or typhoid pneumonia and was placed on a cot in his room.[7]

In the early part of January 1836, Santa Anna's army of 6,500 men and 1,000 horses was on the march toward Texas. The president-dictator, traveling on horseback with a fifty-man escort, was hurrying north to catch up with his army and insisted on heading toward San Antonio. According to José Enríque de la Pena, a lieutenant colonel in the sapper (engineer) battalion and attached to Santa Anna's staff, it was the unanimous advice of all his senior officers that the president-dictator avoid San Antonio and head for Goliad, a key position that would have opened the door to the principal theater of war.[8] In Richard G. Santos' *Santa Anna's Campaign Against Texas* de la Pena is quoted as commenting: "Santa Anna needs a century of instruction to match the wisdom of his senior officers." None of the president's commanders could see any reason for an attack on San Antonio, a garrison without the slightest military or political importance since the defeat of Cós, but the president's pride had been injured when his brother-in-law surrendered, and San Antonio he must have.

The president and his army were running into difficulties. The terrain was arid and largely desert, and the vanguard division of General Sesma and his troops were living largely off the land. In addition, they were having their troubles with the Indians. The Apaches, at peace with Mexico, stole what horses they could. The Comanches, however, presented another problem. They continually harassed the flanks of the division, raiding the wagons and killing any stragglers they might come upon.

The capricious Santa Anna, in his haste, had ignored one of the cardinal rules of successful commanders—always take care of your troops. There was a shortage of surgeons and hospitals, as well as supplies, carts and oxen, and promises of pay for the troops were rarely met. Many of the troops were convicts recently released from Mexican prisons, or other men of low quality.

In the middle of February, the various armies ran into a very fierce norther, marching directly into driving winds and rain. By nightfall, the rains had turned into snow. Officers, men, women camp followers, and boys all gathered around the few fires seeking warmth. The snow kept up all night and by dawn was knee-deep; many horses had frozen to death and all divisions had seen many desertions. As many of those who deserted were ox-cart and mule drivers, soldiers were ordered to take over their duties. Not being used to handling animals, the men did not know how to take care of their new charges; consequently, the animals were often overworked and mistreated, and many of them died due to beatings, starvation, or just plain exhaustion. All of this resulted in serious transportation problems, and various units of the army became strung out over 300 miles. The army's second-in-command, Filisola, and his contingent brought up the rear of the troops. This, of course, made communications between Santa Anna and his second-in-command exceedingly difficult.

In spite of all of these handicaps, Santa Anna and his generals drove their troops hard and on February 23, 1836, the Mexican president entered San Antonio. A sentinel in the tower of the Catholic Church of San Fernando had reported the advance party of the enemy was in sight. Travis sent out John W. Smith and Dr. John Sutherland on a scouting mission. They soon observed the Mexican forces behind Desiderio Hill and hurried back to report. Travis and his men, who had been living in the city and had entertained themselves at a *fandango* the previous night, promptly retreated into the Alamo and barricaded themselves in the fortress.

Travis had been expecting Santa Anna momentarily. Juan N. Seguin, a captain in the Texas army, was one of the few Mexicans who fought with the colonists. He commanded a company of a large number of Mexican scouts, who also acted as cavalry, and had received information from a fellow Mexican in Laredo who had seen some of Santa Anna's army there. He promptly passed the information on to Travis.

6

CAST OF CHARACTERS

On January 24, 1836, Fannin sailed from Velasco embarked for Copano with the four companies of the Georgia Battalion, and Capt. Luis Guerra's Mexican artillery battery. Two days later he was followed by the *Invincible* with Capt. Burr H. Duval's company. On January 28, after a very rough passage, Fannin landed at Aransas Pass and moved from there to Copano.[1]

The *Invincible* brought good news. The schooner *Tamaulipas,* carrying Captains Turner's and Hart's companies of some 100 recruits and loaded with powder, munitions, clothing, and ordnance, would be due at Copano within three or four days. Two other schooners, the *Caroline* and *Emeline,* loaded with provisions purchased by the Texas agents at New Orleans, were expected to arrive at the same time. The brig *Mattawamkeag,* with a battalion of 184 men from New York, was expected momentarily as it was some weeks overdue.

Fannin and his men spent three days unloading the supplies from the ship, and moving them to the old mission at Refugio. He arrived just in time, as those who had stayed behind at Refugio were getting disenchanted with all the waiting around, and were thinking of dispersing.

On February 4, Fannin wrote from Copano of his plans as commander of the Matamoros campaign. Then, on February 6, he received disturbing news from Major Morris, who had gone to San Patricio with the Johnson and Grant parties heading for Matamoros. Morris reported that Gen. José Urrea and his army had reached Matamoros in an invasion of Texas, and that Santa Anna himself with his *Santanistis* was leading a large force heading toward San Antonio.

Then, a few days later, Fannin received further bad news when he learned that the *Tamaulipas* in attempting to sail from the mouth of the Brazos with Captain Turner's two companies and the Texan army's stock of powder, shoes, clothing, and ordnance supplies, had been cast away on the Brazos bar, and that the *Emeline* was also lost in Matagorda Bay with her cargo of flour and corn. The *Mattawamkeag* had been seized as a pirate by the British in the Bahamas and was detained at Nassau for two months. The other provision schooner, *Caroline,* managed to discharge her cargo on February 14 at Cox's Point.

As a result of these mishaps, Captain Turner's men never reached Goliad. The *Mattawamkeag* finally sailed for New Orleans and arrived there February 12, but for some reason the volunteers on board never joined Colonel Fannin.

The colonel started procrastinating. He and his men had been among those most enthusiastic to march to Matamoros and get their share of the "spoils of victory," especially with himself in command of the venture. Perhaps he feared that Grant's popularity among the men would lessen his own prestige, or perhaps he thought it would be the wiser part of valor to forego Matamoros now that he knew Urrea and his forces were there. Whatever the reason, he decided to give up his plan to attack the city. He then marched his force twenty-five miles north to Goliad and quartered his troops in the Presidio La Bahía, some 400 yards from the Mission Espíritu Santo de Zuñiga. At Goliad, Fannin found Capt. Ira J. Westover, of the regular army, in command. There was also Capt. Albert C. Horton's cavalry troop of forty-eight men from Matagorda. As a colonel in the regular army and senior in rank to all others there, Fannin assumed command of both groups of soldiers and the garrison. Once at Goliad, his army started gathering in full force.

As early as February 7, while still at Refugio, Fannin began organizing a regiment from the volunteers there. Although he was a full colonel in the regular army, for some reason he had a vote of the men and, without debate, was elected colonel of the regiment. Maj. William Ward of the Georgia volunteers was elected lieutenant-colonel and second-in-command. To replace Ward as their major, the Georgia volunteers elected Dr. Warren J. Mitchell of Columbus, Georgia.[2]

For Capt. Peyton S. Wyatt of Huntsville, Alabama, it was a different story. He had been in Texas since the previous December with sixty-seven men and first-rate United States muskets, together with a "light" company of nineteen men, with rifles, commanded by Capt. Amon B. King. To date they hadn't seen any action. Wyatt had never been in sympathy with the Matamoros project, and Fannin's latest bit of uncertainty proved to be the last straw. He returned to the United States on recruiting service and took with him—and paid the passage of—a number of his dissatisfied men.[3] King and his men stayed with Fannin.

A roll call of Fannin's forces, considered by units and in the order in which they came to Goliad under his command, consisted of:

1. Capt. Ira J. Westover's company of regulars. These men were mostly of Irish extraction and were from the Irish colonies of Refugio and San Patricio. These were:
   a. Twenty-nine regular infantry enlisted by Capt. John M. Allen from among the survivors of General Mexia's ill-fated Tampico Expedition, which was marched to Refugio under Lt. Francis S. Thornton around January 1, 1836. This was the group that Houston had ordered to return to Goliad on January 19.
   b. The nucleus, around fourteen men, of a company of regular artillery. These were recruited by Westover in the Irish colonies about January 7, 1836.
   c. Eight or ten regulars recruited by Lt. B. F. Saunders at Matagorda during January and sent to Goliad. These men were placed under the command of Westover.
2. A volunteer company of twenty-nine men who were enlisted by Capt. John Chenoweth in December and January, from volunteers who were then, or had been, at San Antonio for the special purpose of garrisoning Copano. They arrived at Copano about January 20 and some of the men later returned to the Alamo and were killed; others went forward, under Chenoweth, on February 26, to guard the Cibolo

crossing on the road to San Antonio. This group joined Neill's forces at Gonzales and did not return to Fannin's command. The remainder transferred to, and were killed with, other companies under Fannin.

3. Six companies that were organized by Grant and Johnson at San Antonio in December 1835 as a nucleus for their proposed expedition to Matamoros. These were:

a. The "San Antonio Greys," under the command of Capt. William G. Cooke, composed almost entirely of men from the Cooke, or Robert Morris, company of "New Orleans Greys." This company had organized in New Orleans the previous October, arrived at San Antonio in November and distinguished itself in battle against Cós.

b. The "Mobile Greys," under Capt. David N. Burke. The nucleus of this company was a group of about thirty men, organized at Mobile early in November 1835 by Travis' good friends, James Butler Bonham, Albert C. Horton, and Samuel P. St. John. Through a combination of delays, this company failed to reach San Antonio until three days after the surrender of Cós. It was subsequently enlarged by several transfers from Capt. Thomas Breece's company of New Orleans Greys.

c. The "Mustang" company of Capt. Benjamin L. Lawrence, a combination of the "United States Independent Cavalry Company," originally from Tennessee, and the mounted portion of Capt. James Tarleton's company of Louisiana volunteers. This company was recruited as the cavalry unit of the Johnson and Grant army; hence the nickname "Mustangs."

d. Capt. H. R. A. Wiggington's company, the core of which was the mounted portion of the Louisville Volunteers, with accretions from broken companies and other groups of volunteers at San Antonio.

e. A company of artillery under Capt. Thomas K. Pearson, who had landed at Paso Cavallo in November with a small company of men, and had aided in the transporting of an eighteen-pound cannon from Dimitt's Landing to San Antonio. This delayed his arrival at San Antonio until three days after Cós surrendered.

f. Capt. Thomas Lewellen's company. This company was composed of men who had served with other companies during the San Antonio campaign, and had re-enlisted for new service after having been discharged with Colonel Burleson's men.

The two companies under Lewellen and Pearson went from Refugio to San Patricio with Grant and Johnson before Fannin reached Refugio and assumed command; hence, they were never regularly enlisted in the service of Texas nor became, except nominally, units of Fannin's command. Capt. Cooke of the Greys followed Grant and Johnson as far as San Patricio with the intention of accompanying them to Matamoros. Once at San Patricio, he had second thoughts on the matter and went back to Goliad. On the other hand, his fellow "Grey," Robert Morris, chose to ride with Grant and Johnson.

4. The four companies of the Georgia Battalion included:
   a. The First Company, under Capt. William A. O. Wadsworth, enlisted at Columbus, Georgia (the home town of Fannin and Mirabeau B. Lamar). This company had been much enlarged by recruiting at New Orleans and en route to Texas.
   b. The Second Company, under Capt. Uriah J. Bullock. This was a section of a very large company enlisted at Macon, Georgia, and vicinity, by Maj. William Ward. When this company left the Brazos on January 24, Bullock was sick with measles and unable to travel. He never rejoined the company or exercised command of it.
   c. The Third Company, under Capt. James C. Winn of Gwinnet County, Georgia. This was the second section of the large company organized at Macon by Major Ward. This company was later augmented at the mouth of the Brazos, while en route to Texas, with various additions, most of whom were volunteers from Mississippi.
   d. The "Alabama Greys," serving under Capt. Isaac Ticknor. These men were recruited by Edward Hanrick at Montgomery, Alabama. This company arrived at Velasco only a few days before Fannin sailed.

5. A company recruited by Capt. Burr H. Duval of Bardstown, Kentucky. He began his journey to Texas in early December 1835 with only six or eight men, but by the time he arrived on the Brazos the last week in December, the group had enlarged to more than twenty.

After Fannin arrived at Goliad he was reinforced successively by:

a. The Alabama "Red Rovers," enlisted at Courtland and Tuscumbia, Alabama, under forty-five-year-old Capt. Jack Shackelford, in private life a physician. This company was armed, as was Capt. Wyatt's company, with muskets borrowed from the arsenal of the State of Alabama, and it received additions after landing in Texas and en route. The company was well commanded and well equipped, and had increased by March 19 to almost seventy men.

b. A squad of ten men, recruited in Tennessee and Mississippi by Capt. John C. Grace, which joined Fannin at Goliad, in company with Shackelford's command.

c. Another squad of eight or nine men sent to Fannin by the General Council from San Felipe on February 9. The squad was commanded by Lt. Samuel Sprague.

d. The Refugio Militia Company under Capt. Hugh McDonald Frazer. This group was mentioned by Fannin as being in active service on February 11 and 12, and consisted of some fifteen or twenty men. Before the actual fighting began, the group was diminished in size by detail as couriers and to care for fleeing families.

e. Capt. Albert C. Horton's company of Matagorda volunteers, forty-eight men in all. This group generally operated out of the Victoria area, and did not join Fannin until after the loss of the Georgia Battalion and Capt. King's men.

f. Among the latecomers to join Fannin were a group of five men who had ridden with Grant and managed to escape from his defeat at Agua Dulce; three who had been at San Patricio with Johnson; and one or more of

Sam Houston's couriers who were captured with
Fannin on March 20 and shared his fate.[4]

Once settled in at the garrison of La Bahía, Fannin completed the reorganization of his regiment and added another
battalion, what was called the Lafayette Battalion, to the Georgia
Battalion, which had already elected their officers. To head the
Lafayette Battalion with the rank of major, Benjamin C. Wallace
from Erie, Pennsylvania, was elected.

Under the new setup, several of the companies were
reduced in size. When he left Refugio on January 21, Sam
Houston had taken Captains Lawrence and Wiggington with
him in order to send them on recruiting service in the United
States. Many men of both their companies, and a number from
Capt. Cooke's, were dissatisfied or ill, and they were released
from service at the same time. Cooke decided to serve under
Houston and went off to join him.

The Lafayette Battalion, as organized by Fannin, consisted
of Capt. David N. Burke's Mobile Greys or New Orleans Greys,
commanded by 1st Lt. J. B. McMonomy. What was left of Capt.
Lawrence's "Mustang" company was consolidated with Burr H.
Duval's company, henceforth called "Duval's Mustangs." The
remnant of Capt. Wiggington's company under Lt. Edward
Fuller was absorbed by what was left of Capt. Wyatt's company,
with 1st Lt. Benjamin F. Bradford in command, and was known
as the "Alabama Greys." After Cooke resigned to go to join
Houston, he was succeeded by 1st Lt. Samuel O. Pettus, another
Virginian, and the company was enlarged by being consolidated
with the small company of Capt. John C. Grace, of Memphis,
Tennessee. This group, formerly the New Orleans Greys,
became the San Antonio Greys. In addition, there were the
Kentucky volunteers, headed by Capt. Amon B. King of
Paducah, Kentucky.

Serving as artillery were Capt. Luis Guerra's Tampico company of Mexican artillerymen, and the Texan regular artillery
from Westmore's command.

When Santa Anna reached San Antonio, the men of
Guerra's company were, at their own request, given honorable
discharges as they explained they did not want to fight against

their own countrymen. They were replaced by a small company of volunteer artillerymen recruited from various other companies, and commanded by Capt. Stephen D. Hurst of Philadelphia. Benjamin H. Holland, engineer and sailor from New Orleans, and four Polish artillerymen under Capt. H. Francis Petrussewicz completed the contingent. John White Bower was director of espionage, and Capt. Frazer's Refugio militia company acted as regimental scouts and spies.

Members of Fannin's staff included Capt. Joseph March Chadwick, a West Pointer, as adjutant, and John Sowers Brooks of Staunton, Virginia, a former Marine served as assistant adjutant and aide. Dr. Joseph H. Barnard, who had joined Capt. Shackelford on his trip to Texas, served as one of the regimental surgeons, while Dr. Joseph E. Field served as the other surgeon. The staff was completed with Capt. Nathaniel R. Brister as assistant adjutant and aide; Gideon Rose, regimental sergeant major; David Holt, regimental quartermaster; Lewis Ayers, assistant quartermaster; and Valentine Bennet, commissary.

Virtually none of the men who served under Fannin and fought for the Texas cause were colonists or old settlers who had come to Texas in an endeavor to make a permanent home for themselves. The majority of his forces had crossed the borders into Texas only a short time before they joined him. He had a few mature and professional men in his ranks, but in the main those serving under him were young boys in their late teens and early twenties. A few were only fourteen or fifteen years of age. The Southern states of Louisiana, Mississippi, Tennessee, Alabama, Kentucky, and Georgia contributed the majority of the troops, although there were some from Ohio, New York and Maryland, and even a few from Germany and Poland.

The fact there were so few "Texans" in Fannin's army was a constant source of irritation to both Fannin and his men, and they would complain about it.

7

DREAMS OF GLORY VANISH

Dr. Joseph Henry Barnard was born in Canada in 1804. After graduation from the Berkshire Medical Institute, he practiced medicine in lower Canada and then moved to Chicago, where he established a practice. Hearing of the Texas Revolution, he closed his practice and on December 14, 1835, left Chicago in company with two other young men to go to Texas and join the Texas army. After voyaging down the Mississippi to New Orleans, he left that city on January 10 on the schooner *Aurora* and several days later landed at Matagorda, a little town of some twenty-five or thirty houses, three or four mercantile establishments, two groceries, and two boarding houses.

It had been the doctor's intention to join the army immediately, but after investigating the situation he decided to postpone his decision. Everything was in confusion and there was no organized army as such. Travis had some troops at San Antonio, Colonel Fannin had a force at Goliad, and a small body of men were at Gonzales. Talk was being bandied about that some troops were to move beyond the Rio Grande to capture Matamoros, "which seemed to [Barnard] wild and visionary, and I felt no inclination to join such an enterprise."[1]

The row between Governor Smith and the General Council was common knowledge and it disgusted Barnard. He spent several days hunting and fishing and in early February found himself at Texana[2] on the Lavaca River. There he found Capt. Jack Shackelford and his Alabama Red Rovers, who had been passengers on the *Brutus* and landed at Matagorda the same day Barnard did. Shackelford and his men had reported to the governor and were awaiting instructions. During the day an order from Acting Governor Robinson came in, instructing Shackelford to report to Fannin at Goliad. Then a courier arrived with news of the approach of Mexican troops, and letters from Fannin for all volunteers to proceed west to Goliad. Barnard liked the looks of the Red Rovers, fine-looking citizens from Alabama and dressed in uniforms of brown hunting vests and trousers. He was impressed with the character, leadership qualities and intelligence of Shackelford, and decided to join his company of seventy men. On February 12, Barnard and the Red Rovers arrived at El Presidio La Bahía del Espíritu Santo, or the "Fort of the Bay of the Holy Ghost."

The Presidio La Bahía was first founded on Garcitas Creek, near Espíritu Santo Bay, in April 1722 but was moved to its present location in 1749. In his journal, as edited and annotated by Hobart Huson, Barnard gives his description of the garrison:

> It is situated on the southwest bank of the San Antonio River, about thirty miles from where (after meeting with the Guadalupe) it empties into the aforesaid Bay of Espirito Santo. It is built upon a rocky elevation and is a good military position. A square of about three and a half acres is enclosed by a stone wall of eight or ten feet in height, the sides facing nearly to the cardinal points. The entrance, or gateway, is about the middle of the south wall. On each side and also along the western wall were rooms built up with it, which served for barracks for the garrison. At the northeast corner of the fort is the church, about eighty-five feet in length by twenty-five feet in width. The walls are built of stone, and are about three feet in thickness. They are carried up about twenty feet when they are turned over in an arch for the roof, which has a parapet around it about four feet in height . . . .
>
> Jutting out from the north side of the church, (which is continuous with the north side of the fort) are two small rooms, each about eight feet square, and on the south side

of the church is another room about twelve feet square. The
door of the church is at the west end, where it opens into a
quadrangle of about fifty feet square, distinct from the main
fort, yet forming part of it, and through which citizens of
the town could enter the church without passing through
the fort.[3]

(Today, just outside the entrance to the quadrangle, is a
cemetery marker covering the grave of Augustus William
Magee, Second Lieutenant, United States Army, 1789, died in
1813, while leading the Magee-Guiterrez expedition—the first
of three expeditions prior to the Texas war of revolution to
declare Texas an independent nation.)

According to Barnard, when he joined Fannin at La Bahía,
the garrison consisted of around 300 men. Now it totaled
around 370. Within a few days, as other units arrived, the roll
increased to around 400. As a group, they came from cultured
families; Burr H. Duval's father was governor of Florida.
According to Barnard the men were, for the most part, "altogether superior to the ordinary material of an army in intelligence and education. They were far from being a class of mer-
cenaries, but were men of character and standing, and some of
them of wealth, who had left their homes from sympathy for a
people who had taken up arms for their liberty."[4]

Unlike frontiersmen, few had had any military, hunting, or
trapping experience. They were adventurous, high-spirited and
enthusiastic, and many had joined the Texan cause to receive
the bounty of land promised them. They were unaccustomed to
discipline and didn't want to meet the demands of rigid military
obedience. Consequently, it didn't take them long before they
got bored with the inactivity of garrison life.

From the first Fannin exhibited a "fortress" mentality once he
settled in at La Bahía. He wasted time—time that could have been
better spent in training his young troops in fundamentals such as
discipline and military tactics and maneuvers, as well as teaching
details of life in Texas such as yoking and driving wild oxen, keeping and riding horses "on the grass,"[5] and strengthening the fort.

Under the supervision of Captain Chadwick, his adjutant,

and with the assistance of Captain Brooks and some Polish engineers, the walls were rebuilt and two trenches four feet apart were dug around them. The old block houses were improved and a new one built. To provide water in case the fort was besieged, a covered walk 200 yards long was constructed to connect the fort with the river. The clever Brooks invented an "infernal machine" consisting of one hundred old muskets, left behind by Captain Collinsworth, mounted in a wooden frame, which could be fired with a single match. In addition, he designed a half-moon battery—a sort of crude early day machine gun—to cover the entrance to the fort. Fannin did spend some time training his raw troops in military tactics, but nevertheless, his army had plenty of idle time on its hands.

In a lottery, the fort was rechristened Fort Defiance—that being the name drawn from a wheel in which the names "Milam," "Defiance," and "Independence" had been placed.

Fannin, upon accepting his commission as a colonel in the regular army, had sworn to follow the lawful orders of the government and his commander-in-chief, Houston. He quickly disassociated himself from both Governor Smith and Houston and from January 20 until March 1, 1836, forwarded many official reports addressed to "His Excellency James W. Robinson Governor and the General Council of Texas."[6]

The absence of bona fide citizens and settlers of Texas from their own first-line of defense was giving rise to comments and complaints from both officers and men at Goliad under Fannin's command, and he agreed with them. As early as February 7 he wrote Lieutenant Governor Robinson that "among the rise of 400 men at, and near this post, I doubt if 25 citizens of Texas can be mustered in the ranks—nay, I am informed, whilst writing the above, that there is not half that number;—Does not this fact, bespeak an indifference, and criminal apathy, truly alarming?"[7] He then added that his men were directing many "just complaints and taunting remarks in regard to the absence of the old settlers and owners of the soil." On February 14, Fannin followed his letter up with another one mentioning how few Texans were in his ranks, and complaining about how many men in his volunteer army were naked and barefoot. The volunteers, he remarked, manifested a "willingness, nay anxiety," to meet the Mexicans, but they also looked to the Texans to turn out en masse to aid them.

The colonel had just cause to complain about the apathy of the Texans during the revolution. Most of the "old settlers" who had been in Texas for a number of years, who owned farms and tilled the soil, had no interest in politics. In general, they believed in the status quo. They did not believe that aggressive action against Mexico was either necessary or desirable. The native Mexicans were almost all in sympathy with the Mexican government and gave virtually no help to the Anglos, both at Bexar and at Goliad.

In 1835 the population of Goliad had been barely 700, and with the outbreak of hostilities there had been an exodus out of town. Some families left Texas, crossed the Rio Grande and went back to Mexico. Others went to various ranches south and east of the town. After Cós surrendered at San Antonio and was on his way back to Bexar—in spite of his parole—as part of Santa Anna's army, some of the Mexicans who had left Texas joined him and Santa Anna's army on its march back to San Antonio. Others, who had gone to their ranches, provided both Santa Anna and Urrea with valuable information. Very few Mexicans stayed behind in Goliad.

When Fannin heard the news that Santa Anna was concentrating troops at Matamoros for an invasion of Texas, he decided to send a detachment to San Patricio to pass the news on to Johnson and Grant, and urge them to return and join his forces. The New Orleans Greys were selected for this mission. When they reached the small hamlet of San Patricio, they were unable to persuade either Johnson or Grant to forego the Matamoros mission, even though the Greys promised if they would return with them, the force would skip Goliad and return directly back to San Antonio. Johnson and Grant allowed the Greys to take two pieces of artillery with them on their return trip to Goliad. The commanders of the Matamoros Expedition then left San Patricio on the long march over the desert leading toward Matamoros and the rich spoils they anticipated.

Upon returning to Goliad, the Greys were unable to march on to San Antonio as they intended, inasmuch as Fannin refused to issue them any provisions. He told them that several ships from New Orleans were expected to arrive at Lavaca Bay in the near future, and that provisions would be available when they arrived.[8]

When Johnson, Grant, and their force of about 100 volunteers who had chosen to remain with them left San Patricio, they spent some time rounding up horses. Previously, Johnson had promised Fannin he would try to capture horses from the Mexican ranchers to mount Fannin's force as cavalry for the intended expedition into Mexico. On their way south they had captured a detachment of Mexican dragoons with about 100 horses for Urrea's army. Johnson proposed that the entire force return to Goliad and give the horses to Fannin; perhaps he and his men would then join them on their march to Matamoros. Grant had a different opinion. He knew of a big ranch nearby that had a large herd of horses belonging to the Mexican government. Perhaps they could round up some of them.

The two men came to an agreement and decided to split their force. Johnson, with thirty-four men, and the 100 horses, would await Dr. Grant and his sixty or seventy men, together with the horses they managed to catch. Upon returning to San Patricio the dragoon prisoners were released on their parole, and promptly returned to Urrea's army.

It was late February 1836, and Urrea and his 1,000-man army were on the march in Texas after passing through Matamoros, where he had augmented his force. The winter had been a particularly severe one; it had been snowing heavily, and the general had lost six men through exposure to the chilling winds and severe temperatures before arriving at San Patricio. As many of the owners of houses in San Patricio had moved to Mexico, their houses were vacant. Johnson and several other men moved into one of the vacant houses, but most of the other men chose to stay in a larger blockhouse. It was nearly freezing outside and none of the men were dressed for cold weather; sentry duty would be highly uncomfortable under those conditions. Deciding to dispense with sentinels for the night—an unwise decision, as it turned out—the men went to bed.[9]

At three o'clock in the morning of February 27, soldiers of Urrea struck the temporary billets and virtually wiped out all of

Johnson's men. The lucky Johnson and a bare handful of men escaped.

Herman Ehrenberg, who survived the massacre at Goliad, later got the story from one of the men with Johnson who managed to survive the surprise attack. According to this source, the house Johnson and his companions were staying in had been surrounded by the Mexicans, who were shouting "down with America," and "death to the Texans." In spite of the heavy firing Johnson and his five friends made a dash for the open through the ranks of the Mexicans. In the confusion, Johnson and four of his men got away safely but one man had been killed. The five survivors then tramped on foot back to Goliad, living only on the fruit of the cactus plant.

Urrea later reported that his men had killed twenty, including Captain Treadway, and captured thirty-two. His own losses, he said, were one dragoon killed and four wounded. After Johnson made his report to Fannin, he started for the Texas army on the Colorado, but when he heard the army was retreating to the Brazos he decided to end his military career. He returned home and "retired to the Trinity."

After the short-lived imbroglio at San Patricio, Urrea sent scouts out to find the whereabouts of Dr. Grant, Major Morris, and their party. Receiving information that Grant was returning to San Patricio, Urrea set out at dark to intercept and surprise him. At a little creek called Agua Dulce, about twenty-five miles slightly southwest from San Patricio, the Mexican commander formed an ambush. He divided his forces into two parties, and on the morning of March 2 completely surprised and defeated the doctor and his force. From then on there is a discrepancy as to what actually happened.

Lt. Col. Enrique de la Pena, the engineering officer attached to the staff of Santa Anna, stated that forty-two men were killed in the engagement at Agua Dulce, including Dr. Grant and Major Morris, and that some prisoners were taken. Urrea, claimed de la Pena, knew that Grant was a prominent man in Mexico. Knowing this, he recommended that no attempt should be made against his life and that every effort be made to take him a prisoner. However, the bait of Grant's silver saddle, of his flashy firearms and other valuable jewels, provoked one of the "cossack" officers to murder him. On many occasions, claimed de la Pena, he heard Urrea lament his death.

According to the military diary of Gen. José Urrea, Grant was wounded in the battle and taken prisoner back to San Patricio, where he spent some time taking care of his own wounds and the wounds of some of his companions. There he was promised that as soon as he and his friends recovered he would be given a passport to leave the country without molestation. However, about three weeks later, when Urrea and his army departed, one of his captains sent eight men in search of a wild horse. When they found one, Grant was brought forth and by the captain's order his feet were strongly bound to those of the horse, and his hands to the tail. "Now," said the captain, "you have your passport—go!" At the same moment, the cords by which the mustang was tied were severed. The fierce animal, finding his limbs unfettered, sprang away with great violence, leaving behind him the mangled remains of poor Grant.[10]

Of the fracas at Agua Dulce, there were seven known Texas survivors who managed to escape back to Goliad with the news of the ambush. They were Capt. Placido Benavides, Randolph de Sprain, William J. Gatlin, David Moses, Reuben Brown, James Reed, and William Scurlock.

Benavides, who was in the advance party with Grant, was a prominent and wealthy Mexican from Victoria who had elected to follow Grant and Johnson on their venture. He stated that Grant ordered him to try to escape and carry the news back to Fannin, which he did. Brown gave an eyewitness account of the action and said he was taken out to be shot, but that a priest and a Mexican woman named Francita Alavez, later to be known as the Angel of Goliad, interposed in his favor and he was spared.

And so, ignominiously, ended the much-vaunted expedition to Matamoros, and the dreams of glory and spoils.

8

GARRISON LIFE

In the beginning, Fannin's troops found garrison life at Fort Defiance very pleasant. There were plenty of provisions, arms and ammunition, and promises of more from Robinson. In addition, almost every man had his rifle and brace of pistols. To complement the standard weapons, all of the New Orleans Greys had brought with them the Bowie knife made famous on the frontier by Jim Bowie.

The novelty of military life was still fresh for the men, and they went about their daily tasks with enthusiasm, while awaiting with confidence the advance of the enemy. But then the garrison began to suffer from a shortage of supplies. Though the cargo of the *Caroline* was landed at Port Lavaca on February 14, and another cargo, which followed, was soon discharged at Cox's Point and Dimitt's Landing, none of those provisions had as yet reached Fannin in larger quantities than an overnight supply. The supply of corn ran out, as did salt. Clothing was wearing out, and some of the men were barefooted as they performed sentry duty.

Many of the young men under Fannin had been highly enthusiastic about the proposed Matamoros Expedition, as they considered it to be a lark and wanted some of the proposed spoils of victory. Now it seemed as if no expedition would take place on Fannin's part, and with little food, poor clothing, and inactivity the troops were getting restless, as armies throughout history have done, and were beginning to grumble. Worse yet, many were beginning to desert. To Robinson, Fannin mentioned "I have been greatly troubled to get my Malitia [militia] to work or do any kind of garrison duty; but I am now happy to say, that I have got them quite well satisfied, and being well disciplined, and doing good work . . . "[1]

The few Mexicans left in Goliad were of little help to the Texans. Although they expressed sympathy with the Texas cause, they pleaded that they themselves were short of clothing and food staples. John Crittenden Duval was a private in the company captained by his brother Burr, and was a survivor of the Goliad Massacre. He later recounted in his book *Early Times in Texas* how his company acquired the nickname "Mustang" and gave a possible reason as to the coolness of the Mexican townspeople.[2]

The company had a second lieutenant, one J. Q. Merifield, who was a physically powerful man. When sober, Merifield was a very peaceful and genial man; but when he was drunk he had the habit of kicking doors from their hinges, which did not endear him to the Mexicans. On one occasion he was so drunk he battered down the doors of half a dozen houses in one street; from then on the Mexicans called him the "Mustang," and eventually the name was applied to the whole company.

Acting Governor James W. Robinson and his fellow armchair strategists, safe in their redoubt at San Felipe de Austin, far away from where the action was, were busy proving their incompetence. Having no idea as to the approach of Santa Anna's army of *Santanistas*, Robinson and the council repeatedly urged the colonel to move on against Matamoros. They promised him aid from the militia and volunteers, and supplies recruited in the United States. On February 13, Robinson wrote Fannin: "You will occupy such points as in your opinion deem best . . . . Fortify and defend Goliad and Bexar and give the enemy battle if he advances. All former orders given by General Houston or myself are countermanded so you may do as you may deem expedient."[3] At the same time, he cautioned Fannin not to risk too much in battle. Robinson signed his letter "Jas. W. Robinson, acting governor and commander in chief of the army." A second letter the same day advised Fannin that neither Bexar nor Goliad would be attacked, as it was thought the Mexicans were too busy fortifying Matamoros against the expected invasion of the Texans. Two days later the Advisory Committee advised Fannin not to make a retreating movement from Goliad, recommending that he maintain control of both Copano and San Patricio.

By now Fannin, who had enthusiastically told Houston earlier that he was more qualified than any other man to be made a brigadier general, was having second thoughts as to his ability. On February 14 he reported to Robinson: "I am not, practically, an experienced commander, . . . I do not desire any command, and particularly that of chief. I feel I know, if you and the council do not, that I am incompetent . . . "[4] He also wrote that during General Houston's furlough he knew that the command "naturally and of right" devolved on him, that he had not been officially notified of that fact either by Houston or the governor. The steps he had taken were those of prudence and for defense, allowable to a colonel of volunteers. He begged for orders and declared that he would obey even if sacrificed. He further wrote: "I am a better judge of my military abilities than others, and if I am qualified to command an army, I have not found it out. . . . I also conscientiously believe that we have none fit for it now in the country . . . with such as have been in the field since October, I do not fear comparison."[5]

Apparently Fannin was having trouble making up his mind as to what to do, as on February 16, while suggesting steps for counteracting the Mexican advance, he asked permission either to take up his headquarters at San Antonio, if Houston did not return at the expiration of his furlough, or to be placed in the Reserve Army. He said that he considered Bexar, Guadalupe (Victoria), and Colorado to be posts of danger and honor. It just didn't occur to Fannin that one of the requirements of a commander is to use his own initiative when the occasion requires it.

Still firing off his broadsides to Robinson, on February 21 Fannin wrote that he had no idea of retreating, nor had he ever had such an idea. Though assuring his soldiers that the Texans would respond to his appeals for aid, and though grateful to the governor and council for the steps they had taken to get the militia in the field, Fannin declared that he was skeptical regarding aid and looked for no considerable force in the field until those there were either sacrificed or forced to retreat.

The fort commander's indecisiveness and constant stream of complaining letters to the government was beginning to affect the morale of his troops. The nearby town of Goliad offered no divertissement, other than a small cantina that the men occasionally patronized, and the few remaining townspeople kept to themselves. Confinement in the garrison was becoming irksome. In spite of the time spent in drilling and refurbishing the presidio, the men had plenty of time on their hands to talk, and talk they did about their commander. Adjutants are not always discreet, and the men in the fortress knew their colonel was complaining repeatedly to the Provisional Government about the insecurity of his position. Men in the ranks invariably respond positively to a commander they have confidence in, and negatively to one they have no confidence in. The troops were beginning to lose faith in Fannin.

With the approach of the Mexican forces at Matamoros, the port of Copano had been abandoned by the Texans. Consequently, from a military point of view, La Bahía had become unimportant as a military post; or, at least, not nearly as important as it had been. With the exception of Captain Westover and his regulars, all the men were volunteers, and they had enlisted with the expectation of seeing some action. With the exception of the few who had taken part in the campaign against Cós at San Antonio, none of those spoiling for a fight had seen any action.

Fannin knew all this but still was in a quandary and didn't know what to do. He had been instructed by Robinson to stay and defend Goliad, and not to retreat. At the same time, he had been instructed by the acting governor to do as he deemed expedient. With little food, clothing, munitions and other military supplies, he was in no condition to leave the garrison and head southeast to meet and attack Urrea in the field. In addition, he very likely knew his forces were vastly outnumbered by those of the Mexican general. He was the man on the scene and logically knew the situation better than anyone at San Felipe, yet he wouldn't use his initiative to abandon Fort Defiance and take his army to either

San Antonio or Victoria. He solved his problem by digging in at the presidio, and waiting for further orders.

By now, appeals were beginning to come in from William (Buck) Travis at the Alamo in San Antonio, begging for help. On February 16, James Bonham arrived as a courier from Travis and spent the day trying to talk Fannin into taking help to the Alamo. Fannin gave him a negative reply.

It seems that the subject of Houston was constantly on Fannin's mind. Although he was always slow to recognize any authority that Houston had, and frequently disobeyed any orders the general gave him, he constantly worried about who was in command of the army. On February 22, once more he wrote the government declaring that neither he nor the army had received information as to who should command the army during the absence of Houston:

> It is my right, and in many respects, I have done so, when I was convinced the public weal required it. I well know that many men of influence view me with an envious eye, and either desire my situation or disgrace. The first they are wel-come to—and many thanks for taking it off my hands. The second will be harder to effect. Will you allow me to say to you, and my friends of the old and new Convention, that I am not desirous of retaining the present, or receiving any other appointment in the army? I did not seek, in any man-ner, the one I now hold, and, you well know, had resolved not to accept it—and but for Colonel Barnet and Clements, and Kerr, would have declined.[6]

Fannin apparently overlooked or ignored the fact that Robinson had written him on the thirteenth, signing himself as commander-in-chief of the army. But worry about the matter he would, although in his position he had much more important things to keep him occupied.

On February 25, once more Bonham came galloping through the gates of Fort Defiance carrying urgent messages to Fannin from Travis, Jim Bowie, and Davy Crockett at the Alamo, stating they were being besieged by Santa Anna and were under constant bombardment. The letters pleaded for help, and once more called upon Fannin to bring his troops to their aid.

A discussion was held with the officers, and Lt. Col. William Ward, Fannin's second-in-command, gave it as his opinion that a portion of the forces at Goliad should be sent to San Antonio since, from the information received, the enemy's largest force would be directed against that place.

The troops, bored with inactivity, were enthusiastic now that they could see some excitement ahead. Fannin's aide-de-camp and engineer, John Sowers Brooks, said that all the force insisted upon going and that none would consent to stay "except the regulars, who wished to go but would obey orders under such circumstances." Capt. Amon B. King's company was recalled from its outpost duty at Refugio to join the main force.

A march at dawn was ordered by Fannin to relieve the Alamo. The evening before, at ten o'clock, Brooks wrote a letter to his father in Staunton, Virginia.

> We will march at dawn tomorrow with 320 men and 4 pieces of artillery,—2 sixes and 2 fours. We have no provisions Scarcely, and many of us are naked and entirely destitute of shoes, and very little ammunition. We are undisciplined in a great measure; they are regulars, the elite of Santa Anna's army; well fed, well clothed, and well appointed and accompanied by a formidable battery of heavy field and battering pieces. We have a few pieces but no experienced artillerists and but a few rounds of fixed ammunition, and perhaps less of loose powder and balls. We can not therefore, calculate very sanguinely upon victory. However, we will do our best, and if we perish, Texas and our friends will remember that we have done our duty . . .[7]

After having finally made up his mind to go to the aid of Travis, Fannin wrote Robinson and the council on February 25 giving an account of expenditures he had made under his authority as agent. He furnished drafts and receipts, and stated the amount on hand was $393.28. He also mentioned that Col. Frank Johnson had never accounted for any of the $2,000 given to him by Fannin.

On the last sheet of his letter he outlined the situation, stating he could not ignore Travis' call for help, and said he was going to his assistance although he realized the venture was a reckless one. "I am aware that my present move toward Bexar is any thing but a military one—the appeals of Cols Travis and Bowie cannot pass unnoticed—particularly by troops now in the field—sanguine, chivalrous volunteers—Much must be risked to relieve the besieged. If however I hear of the fall of Bexar before I reach there I shall retire on this place and complete the fortifications now in a state of forwardness and prepare for a vigorous defense, waiting anxiously in *any event* for the arrival of reinforcements from the Interior."[8]

For some reason Fannin did not move out on February 26 as planned, and for two days the troops fidgeted while their commander wrote more letters. Finally, on February 28, after three days of dragging his heels, Fannin left Captain Westover and his company of regulars, and a battery of artillerymen, at La Bahía to garrison the fort, and started his army on the march heading northwest some ninety-odd miles toward San Antonio. He was realizing the precarious position he was in, and before he started his march he wrote to his friend and partner in a sugar plantation, Joseph Mims:

> The advice which I gave you a few days ago is too true. The enemy have the town of Bexar, with a large force, and I fear will soon have our brave countrymen in the Alamo. Another force is near me, and crossed the Nueces yesterday morning and attacked a party by surprise under Colonel Johnson, and routed them, killing Captain Pearson and several others after they had surrendered. I have about four hundred and twenty men here, and, if I can get provisions in tomorrow or next day, can maintain myself against any force. I will never give up the ship while there is a pea in the dish. If I am whipped it will be well done, and you may never expect to see me. I hope to see all Texans in arms soon. If not we shall lose our homes and must go east of the Trinity for a while. Look to our property; save it for my family, whatever may be my fate. I expect some in about this time by Coagly, and wish you would receive and take care of it. I now tell you, be always ready. . . . If my family arrive, send my wife this letter.

Inquire of McKinney. Hoping for the best, and prepared for
the worst, I am, in a devil of a bad humor.[9]

From the moment it began the march was a farce and
revealed much about Fannin's ineptitude as a commander. There
was virtually no food except a small amount of rice and a small
portion of dried beef, as Fannin later reported to Robinson.
There were no horses for the troops, and many of the men were
poorly clothed and barefooted and still were expected to walk to
San Antonio. There were no horses to draw the artillery, only
oxen, and, of course, oxen were used to pull the wagons. Within
two hundred yards of Goliad one of the wagons broke down and
it then became necessary to double-team the oxen in order to
pull the artillery across the San Antonio River. The river crossing
was an arduous one, but the troops finally got across and camped
for the night. There were still ninety miles to go.

In the morning many of the oxen were discovered to have
wandered off as it seemed to have occurred to no one the previous night to have staked them out. The inexperienced drivers had
simply turned them loose to graze. At the insistence of the officers
commanding the volunteers, a council of war was held. The council consisted of all the commissioned officers under Fannin's command. It was unanimously determined that it was impracticable to
carry on toward San Antonio without the proper supply of provisions and adequate transportation. The officers felt that it was
impossible to reach Travis with their artillery, and that Fort
Defiance might fall into the hands of the enemy with the small
force then guarding the garrison. If that happened, all the
promised provisions that were then at Matagorda, Dimitt's
Landing, and Cox's Point would be lost to the enemy Mexican
forces. With the information from some of Fannin's spies that
Goliad was likely to be attacked, it was decided to return to the fort
and complete the fortifications.

Dr. Barnard, who as a surgeon and member of the regimental staff was present at the council of war, in his journal
described the proposed expedition to San Antonio: "With but
three or four hundred men, mostly on foot, with but a limited
supply of provisions, to march a distance of nearly one hundred
miles through an uninhabited country for the purpose of reliev-

ing a fortress beleagured by five thousand men was madness."
He added that later the men found out the Mexicans were aware
of Fannin's movements and had made plans to attack the army
while it was on the road. He complained that Fannin's venture
would abandon Goliad to Urrea without a blow, as there were
not one hundred men left at La Bahía, and Urrea would have
nothing to do but quietly march in and take possession.

To many of the men in the ranks, who had been at San
Patricio and had wanted to head directly for San Antonio
instead of Goliad, there was much disappointment. Herman
Ehrenberg later wrote in his memoirs:

> Great, therefore, was our surprise when a new command
> directed us to return to our quarters in the fort. The only
> explanation offered us for this sudden overthrow of our new
> hopes was that most of the volunteers in our group were
> against the march to San Antonio and preferred to stay in
> Goliad. How Fannin obtained this information is a mystery
> to us, since he never gave the troops a chance to express
> their opinion about the unexpected reversal of his plans.
> The Greys had no recourse save bitter regret over this
> desertion of their old comrades at such a critical moment;
> for we were helpless without Fannin's support, and as long
> as we could not induce him to go to the rescue of the Alamo,
> we were compelled to share his inaction and isolation.[10]

9

THE GATHERING STORM

William Barret Travis, refusing to acknowledge Robinson as acting governor, was still loyal to Governor Smith and on February 13, 1836, had written him that he expected Texas to be invaded by March 15, and stated that every preparation should be made to receive the enemy. Three days later he wrote Smith again, enclosing a report of Green B. Jameson, who was engineer of the fort, with a plan of the Alamo and declared: "Men, money & provisions are needed—with them this Post can & shall be maintained & Texas (that is) the Colonies, will be saved from the fatal effects of an invasion."[1]

With Smith helpless due to the machinations of Robinson and his cohorts, he was powerless to help Travis. Robinson and his followers were still entranced with their dream of invading Matamoros and did nothing.

When the president-dictator Santa Anna arrived within sight of San Antonio, he had his division rest for about half an hour at the foot of the Alazan Hill, two miles from the city. Then he mounted his horse and started toward the city with his general staff, three companies of light infantry under command of Col. Juan Morales, three companies of grenadiers under command of a Colonel Romero, two mortar pieces, and General Ramirez y Sesma's cavalry. Thinking that Travis and his men had retreated to the Mission Concepción, some two miles south of the Alamo, he ordered Gen. Ventura Mora to gather some troops and take the mission. When one of his colonels, Juan Almonte, told him the mission, with its thick forty-five-inch limestone walls, would be a far more formidable fortress for Travis to defend than the Alamo, *el presidente* was surprised that the Anglos chose to make their stand at the Alamo.

While various units of the Mexican army were getting settled into place, Travis sent out his first call for help. It was to the people of Gonzales, and said: "To Andrew Ponton Judge & to the citizens of Gonzales. The enemy in large force is in sight. We want men and provisions. Send them to us. We want 150 men & are determined to defend the Alamo to the last. Give us assistance."[2]

According to de la Pena, who was present at the Battle of the Alamo as a member of Santa Anna's staff, when the first Mexican troops entered the plaza, they were met by a cannon shot from the Texans' eighteen-pounder. The Mexican artillery commander was immediately ordered to set up two howitzers and to fire four grenades, which caused Travis to raise a white flag. When the firing ceased, Travis sent a written communication addressed to the commander of the invading troops, stating that he wished to enter into negotiations. Santa Anna sent back a verbal answer, stating he would not deal with bandits; they had to surrender unconditionally. He received a prompt answer from Travis; it was another cannon shot. Santa Anna then ordered his troops placed in position, and requested Mora to return from Concepción to the Alamo. He then decided to sit in place while waiting for some of his far-flung straggling units to catch up with him. Then the siege began.[3]

At San Antonio, General Santa Anna, the self-styled "Napoleon of the West," proved himself far inferior in his knowledge of military tactics and strategy than his hero. As there was really no good military or political reason for Travis and Bowie to decide to stay in the Alamo instead of blowing it up as desired by Sam Houston, there was no good military or political reason for Santa Anna to have even gone to San Antonio in the first place.

The would-be Napoleon could more profitably have bypassed the Alamo once at San Antonio and left the approximately 150 troops of Travis and his men dying on the vine.

Without exception, at the beginning of his armies' march into Texas, all of his experienced senior generals, many of whom had served in various wars in Europe, had urged him to make his attack on Goliad instead. There was Fannin with a much larger force than was at San Antonio, supposedly planning to attack Matamoros. But the dictator would not listen to them. He was supreme; Mexico's honor had been outraged when his brother-in-law Cós had been defeated at Bexar, and honor must be revenged. To San Antonio he would head. Then, with thousands of troops at his command, he didn't even bother to bottle up the Alamo tightly so that no one could get in or out. Capt. James B. Bonham, from South Carolina, got into and out of the fortress several times carrying messages pleading for help, and eventually thirty-two men from Gonzales got through Santa Anna's lines and entered the Alamo.

Later, in his diary, staff member de la Pena commented that "Santa Anna needed a century of instruction to match the wisdom of his senior officers."

From the tower of the San Fernando church, the tallest building in San Antonio, the Mexican dictator had flown a long, flapping blood-red banner which could easily be seen from the Alamo. It was a sign that no quarter was to be given. However, for a number of days, there were no serious assaults on the Texans' barricade, as His Excellency was waiting for his heavy artillery to arrive, as well as for some more of his straggling units to catch up with him. During the miserable, cold, rainy weather his troops had encountered earlier in the month, he had been forced to abandon his heavy artillery in the muddy roads. Presently his heaviest weapons consisted of a battery of eight-pounders. The Texans, on the other hand, had an eighteen-pounder and an eight-pounder pointing toward town.

At nine o'clock on the morning of February 24, Santa Anna ordered a frontal advance on the Alamo and commenced firing a battery of two eight-pounders and a howitzer. Two hours later he stopped the firing and with his cavalry reconnoitered the vicinity. Later that day, Travis sent a courier through the lines with a letter to Governor Smith. Addressed "To the People of Texas & all Americans in the world," it read:

Fellow Citizens & Compatriots. I am besieged, by a thousand or more of the Mexicans under Santa Anna—I have sustained a continual Bombardment & cannonade for 24 hours & have not lost a man—The enemy has demanded a surrender at discretion, otherwise, the garrison are to be put to the sword, if the fort is taken—I have answered the demand with a cannon shot, & our flag still waves proudly from the walls—I shall never surrender of retreat. Then, I call on you in the name of Liberty, of patriotism and everything dear to the American character, to come to our aid, with all despatch—The enemy is receiving reinforcements daily & will no doubt increase to three or four thousand in four or five days. If this call is neglected, I am determined to sustain myself as long as possible & die like a soldier who never forgets what is due to his own honor & that of his country. *Victory or Death*.

A postcript was added:

The Lord is on our side—When the enemy appeared in sight we had not three bushels of corn—We have since found in deserted stores 80 or 90 bushels & got into the walls 20 or 30 head of Beeves.[4]

On March 1, 1836, fifty-eight delegates assembled in Washington-on-the-Brazos, a hamlet that consisted of about a dozen cabins, or shanties, and with stumps still standing in what passed for a street. The delegates settled down to business in a crude shelter, an unfinished structure with cloth instead of glass in the windows of a building owned by a gunsmith and part-time Baptist preacher named Noah Byars.

Sam Houston, elected as a delegate from Refugio and returned from his furlough, had arrived a few days earlier. Upon his arrival the delegates present showed him a letter that a courier had just brought in from Travis, who had written it from the Alamo, appealing for aid. For some time during the colonists' troubles with Mexico, Houston had been a moderate and advised caution. Now his mind was made up. His advice was to organize the convention, set up a government, and declare complete independence from Mexico. The delegates followed his advice and on March 2—Houston's forty-third birthday—the declaration was unanimously passed.

Three days later, after Houston had told the convention under what terms he would accept the position, he was elected commander-in-chief of the Texian army, including regulars, volunteers and militia, and was bestowed with all powers given a commander-in-chief. Only one dissenting vote, by Robert Potter, was recorded. The new commander was ordered to establish headquarters, organize the army, and continue in office until suspended by the government.

On Sunday, March 6, the convention was called to order in a special session while Richard Ellis, who had been elected president of the convention, read another appeal from Travis. It had been written three days earlier and had just been received.

Travis mentioned that from February 25 he and his men had been under very heavy bombardment from a distance of 400 yards from the walls of the Alamo, and that during that time the enemy had been encircling the defenders with entrenched encampments on all sides. In spite of that, a company of thirty-two men from Gonzales had answered his previous call, and managed to make their way into his fort. He estimated he was opposed by a force of from 1,500 to 6,000 men, with Santa Anna at their head, and from the rejoicing he heard, he thought a reinforcement of 1,000 men had just arrived to assist the Mexican general.

Although he had written Fannin requesting aid, Travis had to date received none, so he was looking to the colonies alone. He wrote that the "blood-red banner waves from the church of Bejar, and in the camp above us, in token that the war is one of vengeance against rebels; they have declared us as such, and demanded that we should surrender at discretion, or that this garrison should be put to the sword. Their threats have had no influence on me, or my men . . . Victory or Death."

After Ellis read Travis' passionate letter a hush fell in the room, and a delegate proposed the convention be adjourned so all delegates could ride to the relief of the Alamo. Houston opposed the proposal on the grounds that although the delegates had voted for independence, no organization had been formed and no constitution had as yet been written. Any government to be formed, he said, "must have an organic form as otherwise we would be nothing but outlaws, and can hope neither for sympathy nor the respect of mankind."[5] The general then pledged to leave immediately for Gonzales, where he had heard a small corps of militia had formed. He promised the Mexicans would never approach unless they marched over his dead body. "If mortal power can avail, I will relieve the brave men in the Alamo."[6]

Houston then strode from the hall, and accompanied by his faithful aide George Hockley, now inspector-general of the army; aides-de-camp Richardson Scurry and Albert C. Horton, and eighteen-year-old Verne Cameron, who was to serve as his courier, mounted his stallion Saracen to ride to Gonzales, about 115 miles to the southwest.

The pleas of Buck Travis for help hadn't fallen on completely deaf ears. When his letter of February 23, addressed to the *alcalde* of Gonzales, was received, the information it contained was promptly forwarded by Maj. R. M. Williamson, commanding the Rangers, to the governor and council on February 25:

"By express from San Antonio under date of 23rd inst., I have received information that 2,000 Mexicans under the command of Sesma have arrived in Bexar and have taken possession of the public square, compelling the American troops (150) in number, to confine themselves to the Alamo. The American troops are determined to defend the place to the last and have called upon their fellow-citizens for help."[7]

The people of Gonzales heeded the call of Travis and at three o'clock on the morning of March 1 a company of thirty-two young men, many of them married, commanded by Capt. Albert Martin and guided by John W. Smith, slipped through the lines of Santa Anna and made their way into the Alamo. Seven men from Gonzales were already inside the former mission.

For a number of days the firing on both sides was intermittent. Then, on Sunday, February 28, Santa Anna received news that a reinforcement of 200 men was coming to the assistance of Travis by the road from La Bahía. He then dispatched Sesma with some units of cavalry and infantry to intercept the relief force from La Bahía. On March 1 Sesma wrote from the Mission of Espada that there was no enemy, nor traces of any, to be discovered, so he and his cavalry and infantry troops returned to San Antonio.

According to de la Pena, during this time, on the night of February 29, a first-class private who was reconnoitering the Alamo, was picked off by a sniper's bullet and killed. Sporadic firing continued between the Mexicans and the Texans with no one being killed, but on March 2 the Mexicans lost another man when a chasseur drowned in the San Antonio River. Santa Anna then received some of his expected reinforcements when, on the third of the month, the sapper battalions from Aldama and Toluca finally arrived. The president, however, was still awaiting the arrival of his artillery.

Although the *Santanistas* had no officers of the engineer's corps who could estimate the strength of the Alamo and its defenses, as that section of the army was still in Mexico, the sappers were able to estimate the facts, based on their experience. In addition, the local Mexican population who, for the majority, were on the side of their countrymen, were only too happy to give Santa Anna information concerning the strength of the garrison and the shortage and munitions and supplies of the Texans.

Field pieces were now beginning to come in, although the heavy artillery was still not expected for another day or so.

On March 4 a council of war was held in Santa Anna's quarters and it was decided to make the assault on the Alamo. Among those present were Generals Sesma, Cós, and Manuel Fernandez Castrillon, and Colonels Juan Nepomuceno Almonte, Francis Duque, Mariano Salas, José María Romero, and Augustín Amat. Also present was the interim *alcalde* of San Luis. In a discussion on the best way to make the assault on the fortress, Castrillon, Almonte, and Romero were of the opinion that a breach should be made in the walls, and that it would take eight or ten hours to accomplish it.

Four columns were chosen for the attack. The first, under command of General Cós and made up of a battalion from Aldama and three companies from the San Luis contingent, was to move against the western front, which faced the city. The second, under Col. Francis Duque and made up of the battalion under his command, and three other companies from San Luis, was entrusted with a like mission against the front facing the north, which had two mounted batteries at each end of its walls. These two columns had a total strength of 700 men. The third, under command of Col. José María Romero, and made up of two companies of fusiliers from the Matamoros and Jiminez battalions, had less strength, for it only comprised about 300 or more men. This column's mission was to attack the east front, which was the strongest, perhaps because of its height or perhaps because of the number of cannon that were defending it. Three of the cannon in the battery were situated over the church ruins, which appeared as a sort of high fortress. The fourth column, under command of Col. Juan Morales, and made up of over a hundred chasseurs, had the task of taking the entrance to the fort and the entrenchments defending it.

The sapper battalion and five grenadier companies, commanded by Santa Anna, made up the reserve of 400 men; its formation was entrusted to Colonel Amat, who actually led it into combat. There were no field hospitals or surgeons to take care of the wounded.

Although at the council of war all officers agreed with Santa Anna's desire to make an assault on the Alamo, in private some of his officers completely disagreed with their commander. Others made no comment at all as they all knew, from past experience, it was completely useless to disagree with him. He did not want his wishes deviated from, and would brook no opposition to his policies.

Richard G. Santos, in his book *Santa Anna's Campaign Against Texas, 1835-1836,* states that Juan Almonte, who was at the meeting as a member of Santa Anna's staff, kept a diary of the war against the Texans. In his entry describing the council of war and the assault on the Alamo, he made some wry comments concerning his commander-in-chief: "Santa Anna assigned to Cós the post of honor of greatest danger, as leader of the assault. To himself, he assigned the post of greatest safety, to command the reserve, but in the event of the failure of Cós to capture the fort, Santa Anna was to lead the advance. Cós did fail, but his troops were rallied and led not by Santa Anna, but by General Juan Valentin Amador."

By March 3, it was obvious to Travis and his men in the

Alamo that they were doomed. His courier and lifelong friend from South Carolina, James B. Bonham, had returned from Goliad after delivering Travis' plea to Fannin, and it was obvious that no help was coming from that quarter. The thirty-two men who had arrived from Gonzales were all the reinforcements they would receive.

Travis wrote his last letters. The first one reached the delegates assembled at Washington-on-the-Brazos and was read by Richard Ellis to those in the assembly. A second letter was sent to Jesse Grimes: "Let the convention go on and make a declaration of independence and we will then understand and the world will understand what we are fighting for. . . . I shall have to fight the enemy on his own terms; yet I am ready to do it, and if my countrymen do not rally to my relief, I am going to perish in the defense of this place, and my bones shall reproach my country for her neglect."

He wrote a note to Rebecca Cummings, whom he had been courting, and another note to his friend David Ayers, who had been boarding his son Charles: "Take care of my little boy. If the country should be saved I may make him a splendid fortune. But if the country should be lost, and I should perish, he will have nothing but the proud recollection that he is the son of a man who died for his country."

Travis then summoned John W. Smith. Smith, loaded with letters from the defenders to their families and friends, shortly after midnight left the fortress and was the last messenger to leave the Alamo until it fell to Santa Anna's troops.

It may have been after Smith left the fort that Travis, according to legend, called his troops together. With his sword, he drew his famous line in the dirt, asking all who wished to stay in the Alamo and die with him to cross the line. With one exception all did, including the ailing Bowie who, on his sick-bed, asked to be carried over. The one dissenter, Louis Rose, a Frenchman, refused to cross. With the blessing of Travis, he climbed over the walls and through the darkness made his way through the Mexican troops to safety.[8]

10

THE ALAMO FALLS

Santa Anna and his army spent all afternoon of March 5 on preparations for the coming assault, and a general order specified the disposition of the various troops.

In the chilly, predawn darkness on the morning of March 6, various brigades of the Mexican army assembled on the open fields beyond the Alamo. At one o'clock the columns started marching, silently advancing toward the river, which they crossed advancing two men abreast over some narrow wooden bridges. Then, when they had reached a point previously designated by Santa Anna, they came to a halt and kept their silence. Precisely at four o'clock, as specified in the general order of March 5, the various columns of Santa Anna swung into their assault with the regimental bands playing the "*Deguello*," the ancient Moorish bugle call of death signifying "no quarter." Santa Anna and his staff were safely stationed across the river in San Antonio, several yards south of the Alamo.

When the buglers of the *Santanistas* sounded the "*Deguello*" the Mexican artillery ceased firing. When the columns of infantry deployed, advancing with their bayonets drawn, there was a slight mist and at first the columns advanced steadily. Then the guns from the fort opened upon them at point blank range and left a wide path of wounded and dead among the Mexicans. Many of the colonists had "Kentucky rifles," whose steel barrel was four feet long and rifled so as to give the bullet a spiral motion, causing it to take a straight course. Living on the frontier, all the defenders were expert shots and extremely accurate with the weapon up to 300 yards. The remainder of the small arms of the Texans were shotguns, firing buckshot, and they were deadly at close range.

As the first advance of the Mexicans reached the Alamo walls and tried to scale them with their ladders, they were wiped out by buckshot and many were pushed backwards on their ladders, falling on their compatriots' bayonets. The Mexican infantry muskets, predominantly English flintlock rifles firing one-and-a-half-inch balls, and with smooth bores and no rifling, did little damage at long range.[1]

When Cós and his column reached their assigned objective, they were swept back by the shotguns and rifles of the Texans and the four small guns behind the palisade, which extended diagonally outward from the chapel front to the guardhouse. In a disorganized throng they retreated but were rallied by General Amador and by the sheer weight of numbers pushing from behind, went over the wall of the outworks. Santa Anna then ordered Colonel Amat into action with the rest of the reserves, and also ordered into battle his general staff and everyone at his side.

Col. Francisco Duque, while rushing with his men toward the north front, fell after being severely wounded. General Castrillon then assumed command of the column and entered through a breach that had been made several days before during the Mexican cannonade. The columns under the command of Colonels Romero and Morales scaled the western walls, and with so many of the enemy now inside the fortress, many Texans sought sanctuary in the chapel, or ran into various rooms and bolted the doors.

After scaling the walls, some of the troops of Romero and Morales then opened the gates to the Alamo, through which soon came the remainder of Cós' column. The four guns at the palisades were then captured and turned upon the front doors of the chapel. The Mexicans, with their overwhelming numbers, then battered down doors of the rooms the Texans had barricaded themselves in, and a terrible hand-to-hand fight began.

The Texans defended themselves with knives and by using gun butts as clubs, while the Mexicans fired at close range and stabbed with their bayonets, not only killing the defenders but mutilating their bodies as well. Bowie, who had killed several Mexicans with his pistol and his famous knife, had been killed in his room while on his bed.

Mrs. Susannah Dickinson, wife of Capt. Almeron Dickinson, the Texans' master of ordnance, had chosen to stay in the Alamo along with her husband and her baby daughter. According to her, after killing Bowie, the Mexican soldiers had tossed his body aloft on a dozen bayonets and then killed John, his black slave.

Finally, by six o'clock in the morning, the carnage was over. Travis, Bowie, Bonham, Crockett, and all the other gallant defenders of the Alamo had passed into Texas history. Santa Anna then entered the Alamo and in a speech before his crippled battalions, lauded their courage and thanked them in the name of their country.

Incredible as it seems, some seven men, among them the famous Davy Crockett, who had been in Texas barely a month, survived the bloody battle. General Castrillon had the men brought before Santa Anna and tried to intervene for them. Santa Anna then severely reprimanded Castrillion for not having them killed on the spot, and personally ordered their execution.[2] Some of the sapper officers, perhaps to flatter their commander, with their swords fell upon the victims with savage ferocity and killed them, horribly mutilating them in the process. Santa Anna then ordered the 188 bodies of the Texans stripped, subjected to brutal indignities, and then thrown into heaps and burned.[3] After viewing the bodies, Santa Anna greeted Capt. Fernando Urizza and commented: "It was but a small affair."[4]

To the Mexican dictator the fall of the Alamo might have been a small affair. But the Texans lost 188 men from seven different nations and twenty-two states, including Texas. The roll-call included seven Mexicans born in San Antonio, and one from Laredo.[5] At the express orders of the dictator, the lives of Mrs. Dickinson, her fifteen-month-old daughter Angelina, and Joe, a black slave of Travis, were spared so they could take the news of the fall of the Alamo directly to General Houston. Also spared were Mrs. Gregorio Esparza, whose husband had fought with the

Texans and perished, and her four children. Two young sisters, relatives of Jim Bowie's wife, Ursula, along with the eldest sister's eighteen-month-old son, were also spared. Santa Anna also spared others of Mexican descent: Trinidad Saucedo and Petra Gonzales. José María (Brigido) Guerrero, who was a Mexican defender of the Alamo, escaped death by convincing the dictator he was a prisoner of the Texans.[6]

Gregorio Esparza had reached his thirty-fourth birthday on the fourth day of the siege. His brother Francisco, who fought with Santa Anna, recovered Gregorio's body and had it buried in the *campo santo* (cemetery). Thus, Gregorio was the only one of the Alamo defenders who was given a Christian burial.[7]

Francisco Antonio Ruiz was *alcalde* (mayor) of San Antonio and witnessed the storming of the Alamo. He later gave an account of the events. When the battle was over and the smoke from the blazing guns had cleared, Santa Anna ordered all the Mexicans taken out. He then ordered wood to be brought to burn the bodies of the Texans, and Ruiz and a company of dragoons foraged wood and dry branches from the neighboring forest.

The defenders of the Alamo were placed on layers of wood and dry branches, and about five o'clock in the evening all the piles were lighted. According to Ruiz, the number of men burned totaled 182.[8] Then, he stated, the dead Mexicans of Santa Anna were taken to the graveyard, but inasmuch as there was not sufficient room for all of them, he ordered the other bodies to be thrown in the river.

Santa Anna's official report of March 6, 1836, listed 600 Texans killed and Mexican losses as seventy dead and 300 wounded, including two commanders and twenty-three officers. However, the tabulation compiled by General Andrade showed Mexican losses as eight officers dead and eighteen wounded, with 252 soldiers dead and thirty-three wounded, a total of 311.[9]

After the fall of the Alamo Santa Anna stayed in San Antonio for several days, still waiting for various units of his army to catch up with him. On March 8, Gen. Antonio Gaono arrived with the remainder of the First Brigade, followed the next day by Maj. Gen. Vicente Filisola, Santa Anna's second-in-command. It is easy in hindsight to criticize how a commander fights his battle, especially if he wins. The quartermaster, Gen.

Juan José Andrade, and his brigade arrived on March 10, and on the eleventh Gen. Eugenio Tolsa showed up with his Second Infantry Brigade.

Santa Anna often referred to himself as "The Napoleon of the West," but it is doubtful if his idol would fight a major battle without having all of his troops in place, and his second-in-command nearby.

On March 11, General Ramirez y Sesma started marching toward Gonzales, taking with him 700 infantrymen, two field pieces with their crews, 100 horses, fifty cases of rifle ammunition, and food for fifteen days. On the same day Col. Juan Morales started marching toward Goliad to reinforce Gen. José Urrea. He took with him a twelve-pounder, an eight-pounder, and a howitzer, together with sixty-five cases of rifle cartridges. For his part, the Napoleon of the West, convinced the war was over, planned to return to Mexico City as he had learned that rebellion had broken out in Mexico.

Before leaving for the Mexican capital, Santa Anna outlined his plan of war to his commanders. It called for total devastation of Texas as homes and farms were to be burned and plundered and civilians stripped of their possessions. All rebels found with weapons were to be executed, regardless of whether they surrendered or not, as this was part of the dictator's scheme to force the Texans to flee east across the Sabine River back into the United States. This strategy was to be carried out by all the dictator's three divisions. To be in overall command during his absence, the dictator selected General Filisola. General Sesma was to command the division in the central zone and after routing the Texans at Gonzales was to proceed to Lynch's Ferry, at the junction of the San Jacinto River and Buffalo Bayou, thence to Anahuac, while General Gaono was to proceed through Bastrop and Washington-on-the-Brazos to Nacogdoches. General Urrea was already on the move up through the coastal area from Matamoros. The combined forces of the armies would total about 6,000 men.

Back at Fort Defiance after his aborted mission to relieve Travis, Fannin continued his practice of sending out a stream of letters. To a friend, he wrote giving some indication of his state of mind concerning his difficulty in receiving any assistance from the people of Texas and his government.

> I have not so much confidence in the people of Texas as I once had. They have been entreated to fly to arms and to prevent what has now been done. I have but three citizens in the ranks and tho' I have called on them for six weeks, not one arrived, and no assistance in bringing me provisions, even Texas refused me. I feel too indignant to say more about them. If I was honorably out of their service, I would never re-enter it. But I must now play a bold game. I will go the whole hog. If I am lost be the censure on the right head, and my wife and my children and children's children curse the sluggards forever.[10]

He followed that letter up with one to Acting Governor Robinson under date of February 29, giving the strength of Fort Defiance as 420 men. He was undecided whether to remain at the fort or to withdraw. "In case immediate reinforcements are not sent to this place and Bexar, I would recommend that the Army of Reserve be concentrated near Gonzales and Victoria, for in that neighborhood must the enemy be met and driven back, if possible. We want your orders, and be assured, that they shall be obeyed to the letter," he wrote.[11]

On the first of March Fannin again wrote Robinson:

> I again repeat to you, that I consider myself bound to await your orders. I can not, in a military point of view, be considered now as acting commander-in-chief, as I have never received orders to that effect, nor has the army. Again, I received furlough to the first of April. Again, I am chosen Commander of this Regiment of Volunteers. Lastly, I have orders from you not to make a retrograde movement but to wait orders and reinforcements.[12]

Apparently, it never occurred to Fannin that at some point a commander must use his own initiative and act on his own.

Fannin then urged that his stores on Matagorda Bay be protected, that his name be erased from the list of officers or expectants for office, and that leave be granted him to bring off his brave volunteers in the best manner he might be able. He mentioned that he now had enough beef for twenty days and hoped to have coffee, clothing, and ammunition soon. It would be the tenth of the month before he had an ample supply of provisions.

Perhaps Fannin was greatly interested in who the commander-in-chief was because he thought the order to retreat should come from him, or from the council under whose direction he had undertaken the Matamoros Expedition. His indecision and inability to act on his own was to prove costly to him and the men under him.

Robinson answered Fannin's letter on March 6 and gave a very inconclusive reply. When the convention had assembled at Washington on March 1, Robinson and his followers, who had taken over the government and done nothing at all constructive, were ignored by the delegates and Robinson was given no position in the new government. He complained about the political infighting going on, and mentioned that Sam Houston had been elected commander-in-chief of the Army of Texas Militia and Volunteers. He added that a thirty-man group had gone from Gonzales to San Antonio to aid Travis and his men, and that more were on their way under Colonel Burleson. He advised Fannin to "do what you can with what you've got. Unless Houston tells you differently, make up your own mind and do it your way."[13]

At last Fannin had finally found out who the recognized army commander-in-chief was.

When the men in the garrison of La Bahía heard the news that a declaration of independence from Mexico had been declared, and an ad-interim government been formed, they cheered. Although the day was stormy, they finally succeeded in hoisting the Lone Star flag of the new republic.[14]

Capt. Luis Guerra and the men under him in his artillery command, from Tampico, were not overjoyed at the news of the declaration of independence. They were ready to help the Anglos fight for the Constitution of 1824, but were not agreeable to fight for the separation of Mexican lands from the Republic of Mexico. They felt it would be disloyal to their own people. Guerra then approached Fannin to let him know how he felt about the matter, and asked to be released from Texas service. Fannin, after thinking it over, agreed and gave Guerra and his men an honorable discharge and passports to New Orleans. Then, on March 11, he wrote Gen. José Antonio Mexia at New Orleans concerning Guerra, and made some comments about Santa Anna and his troops being in San Antonio. Apparently, he had not yet heard as to its fall. Then he wrote a paragraph showing his state of mind at the time:

> I know not how long I may remain in the service—circumstances unexpected and over which I had no control, have placed me, where I cannot retreat, but in disgrace—This I am not disposed to suffer—rather preferring to encounter death in any shape—if I had men, over whom I could exercise reasonable authority, I should glory in the present opportunity as I should most certain do myself some credit, and the Country great service; and teach Genl.Sa.Anna a lesson, which he might remember, and the State of Mexico profit by . . .[15]

As soldiers invariably do when they are bored and have time on their hands, the troops wrote letters. On March 2, 1836, the twenty-two-year-old John Sowers Brooks wrote his mother that "the war is to be one of extermination. Each party seems to understand that no quarters are to be given or asked." He also remarked "we have nothing but fresh beef without salt—no bread for several days."

Ruth Cumby Smith, in her article in volume 23 of the *Southwestern Historical Quarterly,* mentioned that Brooks wrote his sister Mary Ann and said that it had been four months since he had heard from home, and gave an idea of how conditions were in the fort: "I am nearly naked, almost barefooted, and without a cent of money. We have had nothing but beef for several days. We suffer much and labor hard in repairing the Fort."

Dr. Barnard, in his diary, mentioned that the signs of coming danger began to produce a feeling of anxiety, which was further increased by many vague and groundless rumors that circulated among the men, and the restraints of discipline produced discontent and murmurs and a loss of confidence in their commander. Fannin was not slow to notice the feeling of the men, and it caused a corresponding depression in his mind.[16]

Capt. Burr H. Duval, commanding a company from

Bardstown, Kentucky, wrote his father on March 9 with mixed feelings:

> I have never seen such men as this army is composed of —
> no man ever thinks of surrender or retreat. They must be
> exterminated to be whipped. Nothing can depress their
> ardor. We are frequently for days with nothing but bull beef
> to eat, and, after working hard all day, could you at night
> hear the boys crowing, gobbling, barking, bellowing, laugh-
> ing and singing, you would think them the happiest and
> best fed men in the world.[17]

And then he continued: ". . . much dissension prevails among the Volunteers. Col. Fannin . . . is unpopular—and nothing but the certainty of hard fighting, and that shortly, could have kept us together so long."[18]

Fannin was now discovering what many more capable commanders than he had discovered long before: that it is very lonely at the top.

11

FANNIN SPLITS HIS FORCES

While on the road to Gonzales, Sam Houston and his aides were delayed by cold, rain, muddy roads, washouts, and swollen streams. The little band passed many fugitives who had abandoned their homes and were fleeing eastward, panicked by Santa Anna's advance from the south. Houston later wrote: "None turned about, joined our party and faced the hazards of the westward journey."[1] He took with him, however, the knowledge that from that time there was no question that he was the undisputed commander-in-chief of what armed forces the Texans could muster.

After crossing the Colorado River on March 9 and while still on the road to Gonzales, Houston called for Verne Cameron, his young courier. Via Cameron, Houston forwarded Fannin copies of the proceedings of the convention in San Felipe and told him of his election as commander-in-chief of all forces.

By now it was well known that both Johnson and Grant had been wiped out at San Patricio and Agua Dulce, and it was feared that the defenders of the Alamo had suffered the same fate. Houston ordered Fannin to give up the fort at Goliad and to meet him with all available troops on the west side of the Cibilo, about twenty-five miles east of San Antonio. It was Houston's intention to join the force at Gonzales with Fannin's men, with a view to relieve the garrison at San Antonio. Then they would meet Santa Anna in the field.

Houston rode into the volunteers' camp at Gonzales, some seventy-five miles due east of San Antonio, on March 11 about four in the afternoon. There he found 374 men, fifty of whom were mounted. Among those present were James C. Neill, former commander at San Antonio, who had been prevented by the presence of Santa Anna's troops from rejoining the forces at the Alamo at the expiration of his leave. Also present were Capt. Sidney Sherman and his troops from Kentucky and Ohio, who had just marched more than 400 miles from Natchitoches in Louisiana.

The volunteers, under the command of Ed Burleson, were in a pitiable state. Both weapons and ammunition were scarce and the men had provisions for only two days. Houston had Burleson parade the troops. He then read them the Texas Declaration of Independence, his commission, and the new government's instruction to him as commander-in-chief. He realized he was in a delicate situation. In all of Texas this small force was the only army under his direct command, and they had not volunteered to serve under him but had volunteered to defend the Alamo. To be effective, they must be organized into military units with discipline and training.

Shortly after dark on the day of Houston's arrival, two Mexicans arrived at the camp with the terrible news that the Alamo had fallen on May 6, after a siege of thirteen days, and that all of the defenders were dead. Houston then sent Capt. Francis J. Desauque to ride immediately to Fannin at Fort Defiance.[2] In his saddlebags he carried two messages. One was a letter telling Fannin about the fall of the Alamo and the fate of Travis and his men. The other message was an army order addressed to Fannin. It read:

> You will as soon as practicable after the receipt of this order fall back upon Guadalupe Victoria with your command and such Artillery as can be brought with expedition. The remainder will be sunk in the river. You will take the necessary measures for the defense of Victoria, and forward one-

third the members of your effective forces to this point, and remain in command until further orders. Every facility is to be rendered to Women and children who may be desirous of leaving that place. Previous to abandoning Goliad, you will take the necessary measures to blow up that fortress and do so before leaving its vicinity—the immediate advance of the Enemy may be confidently expected—as well as a rise of water—prompt movements are therefore highly important.[3]

Two days later, Houston followed up his orders to Fannin with a letter to James Collinsworth, chairman of the Military Committee of the new government. To Collinsworth, he enclosed a copy of his letter to Fannin to blow up his fortress and go to Victoria, and gave as his opinion "we cannot maintain siege in any fortresses, in the country of the enemy. Troops pent up in forts are rendered useless." As for Fannin, he said, "I could not rely on any cooperation from him."[4]

The troops under Fannin were restless and eager for a fight. Like their commander, they had faith in their fortress and its ability to withstand an attack. Ruth Cumby Smith, in volume 23 of the *Southwestern Historical Quarterly*, stated that young John Sowers Brooks, on March 10, wrote his father that the men were expecting Santa Anna to detach 1,000 men from San Antonio to join with Urrea's 650 men from San Patricio. "We have strengthened the fort very much," he wrote "and he will find with his 1,650 men to drive us from our post."

Brooks then told his father the men were hourly anticipating an attack but were preparing for it. The shortage of provisions was their deadliest foe, and unless they were soon supplied they could not hold out much longer. He mentioned they had had no bread for some time, and he needed shoes and clothing but had no money to buy them. He was writing in haste as "I have just returned from a weary and unsuccessful march in pursuit of a party of Mexicans, who appeared a few miles from this place." In a postscript, he stated the government furnished the men nothing—not even ammunition.

Fannin's army, at this time, was virtually blind as he was suffering from a lack of intelligence. He had no cavalry, and it would be several days before Albert C. Horton and his cavalry would arrive. Santa Anna's troops not only had mounted men covering every road observing the colonel, but his troop commanders had their information augmented by Mexicans friendly to the Mexican cause.

Urrea's army was known to be in San Patricio, but how many troops did he have with him? Fannin thought there were 650 of them but wasn't sure. Then Jesus Cuellar, *"El Comanche,"* arrived on the scene. Cuellar, who had been of so much help when the Texans defeated Cós at San Antonio, presented a plan that would lure Urrea and his advance troops to the Arroyo de las Ratas, some twenty-five miles away from San Patricio on the road to Refugio. Cuellar was confident Fannin's troops could ambush Urrea in the arroyo and destroy them and then move on to San Patricio to pick off the rest of Urrea's army piecemeal. This would give Fannin's troops some of the action they craved. Cuellar promised he would ride to Urrea and lure him into the trap. His brother Salvador, who was with the general, would vouch for his loyalty to the Mexican cause.

Cuellar left, and then returned to Fannin and told him all was in readiness and the trap was baited. Fannin, after thinking things over, did nothing.

Col. Francisco Garay, with Urrea, confided to his diary that Cuellar appeared before Urrea and was vouched for by his brother. Cuellar told Urrea that Fannin was planning to attack him, but if Urrea would go to the Arroyo de las Ratas he could hide in the brush and ambush Fannin. Urrea fell for the plan and started off early in the morning of March 8 with 200 men, 150 cavalry, and one cannon. When they reached their destination Cuellar disappeared, and Urrea then arranged a small force to carry out his plan.

After looking the situation over, Urrea decided it would be difficult indeed to surprise Fannin in that spot. The woods where his troops were to hide were extremely sparse and all the trees were dry and devoid of foliage. The front, left, and rear were immense plains with not even a blade of grass, while the creek was dry and so shallow that it did not cover the infantry placed in it. Urrea realized what a disadvantageous position he was in as Fannin would have detected his army long before they approached, and at midnight ordered a retreat to San Patricio.

Fannin had finally received the orders from the higher authority he had been looking for, giving him instructions as to what to do. In spite of the unequivocal orders from Houston to retreat, Fannin, the Master of Indecision, still procrastinated. Later on, in his report of the campaign, Houston said that to his order of March 11 "he received an answer from Colonel Fannin, stating that he had received his order; had held a council of war, and that he had determined to defend the place, and called it Fort Defiance, and had taken the responsibility to disobey the order."[5]

Fannin not only procrastinated, but he also committed another serious blunder. He split his troops.

It all began with a man named Lewis Ayers, who had been in Texas since 1834 and had formerly lived in San Patricio. In the early part of January 1836, he and his family had moved to Refugio. When the news of the slaughter of the troops led by Johnson and Grant had reached Refugio, most of the Irish colonist settlers, convinced the town would be struck by General Urrea and fearful for their lives and properties, had fled to the east joining others in what became known as "The Runaway Scrape." Ayers and a few other families had no transportation and therefore stayed in Refugio. Then along came David Moses, who was one of the few lucky survivors of Grant's defeat at Agua Dulce. As Moses was on his way back to Goliad to rejoin Fannin, Ayers went along with him to ask the colonel for assistance in moving his family and the others at Refugio to a safer location.

Some of the long-promised provisions of supplies had finally arrived at Lavaca, and Fannin had sent some men and a number of wagons there to pick them up. The carts returned on the night of the tenth, and the next morning Fannin ordered Capt. Amon Butler King, a former town marshal, to take the carts back to the mission, as Refugio was known, and to escort the remaining families there back to Goliad. King started off with some twenty-eight to thirty men of his company from Paducah, Kentucky.

When King and his men arrived at Refugio, they found a number of families gathered around the old mission that was still standing. Ayers and his family, and a Mrs. Hill and her two children, were at the Lopez ranch, about two miles from Refugio and on the other side of Mission River. A widow named Sabina Brown lived near the mission, and in her memoirs she related the first evening King and his men were there: "When at supper time they heard that there was a band of enemy on a ranch ten or twelve miles below the Mission, they said to one another, 'Jolly, now for a fight; maybe they will come tonight;' but morning came, and no Mexicans, much to the disappointment of the Texans, who were starving for a fight. And they began clamoring, 'if they can't come here, we can go there,' and away they went."[6]

The small band of Texans arrived at the Lopez ranch to help the Ayerses evacuate, and found six Mexicans. Five of the Mexicans were pointed out as part of a band of looters who had been plundering the deserted homes and businesses. King and his men captured five of the six, then decided to go to the lower Lopez ranch where, he had been told, there was another group of the locaters. Leaving a small detachment to help the refugees load their possessions, he and about eighteen or twenty men rode to the lower Lopez ranch in search of the looters.

When King and his detachment arrived at the lower ranch, they ran into the looters and an ambush set up along the road by an advance party of Urrea's cavalry, including some Indian troops. A Mexican boy who had marched with King to Refugio had deserted and run to the looters to tell them King was in the vicinity and how many men were with him. King and his men then made a strategic withdrawal without losing a man, and fled back to the Lopez ranch. There they helped their companions load the wagon carts full of furniture and belongings, and with the women and children on top of the carts the wagon train headed back to the mission. Urrea's men promptly followed and caught up with the caravan while they were crossing the Mission River. In the gunfire, one of the women was hit and suffered a broken arm.

King and his men fought back valiantly under the cover of the riverbank and kept their attackers under fire while the colonists reached the mission, which was enclosed with a stone wall several feet high. The Texans then managed to get into their fortress, while the Mexicans and their Indian allies surrounded the church and started a siege, continuing their gunfire. During the exchange of shots a Mexican named Rios raised his head behind the carcass of his horse, which had been shot. A Texas rifleman promptly shot him through the head, killing him.

Sporadic gunfire continued for the rest of the day. That

night one of the boys from Refugio managed to slip through the lines and headed for Goliad with a message calling for help. He arrived there on the morning of the thirteenth. Fannin then sent his second-in-command, Lt. Col. William Ward, from Georgia, with a battalion of 120 men to go to the relief of King. Ward and his men left La Bahía at three o'clock that same morning. The day was wet and it took Ward and his men until after sundown to march the twenty-five miles to the mission, where they ran into the Mexicans. Sabina Brown described it: ". . . arrived at the mission that night between sundown and dark. At the head of a little gully that puts out from the river above the church, the Mexicans had a camp, and Ward and his men, who were called the Georgia Rattlers, ran into this camp, unexpectedly, and then the row began. They drove the Mexicans back to the river in a panic, and a horse with a saddle on ran very nearly into the church and disturbed the families who were cooking their supper."[7]

Ward had been under orders to return promptly to Goliad, but the long march and the brief conflict had tired his men. He decided to let them rest for the night and return to Fort Defiance in the morning with the colonists. But then an unexpected event took King and some of the men away from the mission again.

A little before midnight, a strange fire was seen about a mile down the river in the direction of a ranch. King called for volunteers to go investigate. Capt. Isaac Ticknor with his Alabama Greys, and Capt. Benjamin Bradford with his Alabama company, soon had thirty men under arms.

The men moved out silently along the edge of the woods until they were opposite the fire which was in the prairie about 150 yards from the timber. As it was extremely dark, they managed to creep quietly until they were within forty yards of a party of some seven or eight Mexicans and three Indians. At a given signal thirty rifle bullets killed all of the group.

Early the next morning a small party went out to verify the result of their night's action. Among the dead they found Capt. Luis Guerra, one of the survivors of the Tampico Expedition, and until recently the officer in charge of Fannin's artillery. Another body was that of a Mexican lieutenant named Blanco. He, with Guerra, had joined Fannin at Velasco as a friend to the

Constitution of 1824, and along with Guerra had left Fannin with a passport ostensibly to go to New Orleans. Instead both of them had promptly gone to serve under Urrea.

Urrea, after destroying Grant at Agua Dulce and Johnson at San Patricio, was advancing toward Goliad via Refugio. His spies had told him that Fannin was going to the aid of Travis at the Alamo, so he had sent Capt. Rafael Pretalia with a small party of soldiers and about thirty Mexican civilians to advance and delay Fannin until he could get there with his main force and do battle.

It was this group that King and his men had fought at the lower Lopez ranch. Guerra, Blanco, and their companions were ahead of the lines when they decided to camp for the night.

When the bodies of the dead were searched, the Texans found on them some 510 doubloons, some splendidly wrought Mexican blankets, some jewelry, firearms, and other articles. Among the papers found on Blanco were documents which proved he had been in correspondence with the Mexican army while serving under Fannin's command.[8]

King and his men then returned to the mission.

12

ACTION AT REFUGIO

It was the morning of March 14, 1836. Ward was preparing to march back to Goliad with his troops and caravan of colonists, and Fannin was anxiously awaiting their return. On the same day, Col. Albert C. Horton, who had ridden with Houston to Gonzales, reported in with a cavalry force of fifty-two men from Matagorda and the lower Colorado. He also brought with him several carts and teams of oxen.

A sentinel at Refugio reported to Ward sighting a number of Mexicans in the area. Ward assigned Maj. Warren J. Mitchell to lead a scouting party. King, then, on his own, also set out with a number of men on a reconnaissance. Finding nothing, he decided to return to the mission. Approaching the church he ran into unexpected trouble. While he had been gone, Urrea, with a force of 100 horsemen and 180 infantry, was hurrying to the old church to catch up with Captain Pretalia and his cavalry.[1]

Ward and his men were already safe inside the church. Noting that Pretalia had a relatively small force, they left their sanctuary and attacked, hoping to drive Pretalia off until King and his men returned. Pretalia then retired only a short distance, and the two sides kept firing at each other. Shortly after that the main force of Urrea arrived, and the combined force then laid siege to Ward, who had retreated into the crumbling ruins of the old stone building.

This, then, was the scene when King arrived back near the rear guard of Urrea at the mission. King made a hasty retreat, eventually ending up in some woods six or seven hundred yards away, where a creek and heavy brush made them less accessible. During the rush to the woods, a number of King's men became separated from their friends and five were shot and killed. Two of King's men were taken prisoner.[2]

Urrea at first sent Col. D. Gabriel Nunez with part of the reserve cavalry to dislodge King but was unsuccessful. He then sent a party of sixty infantry under the command of Col. Francisco Garay to accomplish the task. After some fierce fighting eleven of King's men were killed and seven taken prisoner. Then the darkness of the night prevented any further fighting.

During the night King and his men tried to escape. They had expended most of their ammunition the previous evening, and while crossing the nearby river they had gotten all of their rifles and ammunition completely soaked. In the almost total darkness the men got lost. All night they wandered in a circle, and in the morning found themselves back near the mission. They headed for Goliad, but knowing the main La Bahía road leading there would be well patrolled, avoided it. Then their luck ran out.

Carlos de la Garza, although a Mexican born in Goliad, had remained loyal to the cause of Santa Anna. He owned a ranch in the neighborhood of Refugio and had enlisted a number of fellow Mexicans in what he called Captain de la Garza's Victorian Guards. He and his fellow *rancheros* knew the neighborhood thoroughly, and had little trouble tracking King down. With little ammunition, and what they had being wet, King and his men had no choice but to surrender.

Garza and his *rancheros* had been preparing to shoot King and his fellow prisoners on the spot where they had surrendered. German-born Juan José Holsinger, a colonel of engineers under Urrea, arrived on the scene and persuaded Garza to spare the lives of two German-born boys in the detachment. He argued the two lads were good gunsmiths and he could use them. One of them was so badly wounded that he died shortly thereafter, but the other one joined the Mexican army.

Garza and his Victorian Guards then tied King and his companions on one rope, all in a row, and marched them to the church. After half an hour they were marched up the La Bahía road to the slope of the hill below the graveyard, and all were shot.[3]

Although the mission that Ward and his Georgia Rattlers had retreated into was virtually in ruins, with crumbling walls and sagging roof, it was strong and offered good defense. One side was a stone wall 150 feet in length, used as a place of burial and containing many tombs; from the end of this wall the ground descended. Capt. Munroe Bullock's company of thirty-five men positioned themselves in the churchyard to protect the mission from an assault in that direction. The remainder of Ward's command barricaded the church, made holes to fire from, and prepared their defense.

All day of the fourteenth there was constant firing from both sides. Urrea ordered some of his cavalry to dismount and act as infantry with the Yucatan Indians. Then the foot cavalry and the Indians, accompanied by the fire of a four-pounder to batter down the door, made two infantry charges against the church and were repulsed both times by the accurate fire of the frontiersmen defending the building.

According to Urrea, his losses for the day were six infantry and five dragoons killed, and twenty-seven infantry and ten dragoons wounded.[4]

At the end of the day Ward was running low on ammunition. He sent two couriers, one a Cpl. James B. Murphy of Milledgeville, Georgia, to go to Fort Defiance and ask Fannin for ammunition and more men. Both couriers were quickly captured within sight of the mission.

Fannin had been sending messengers to Ward with orders to leave Refugio and return to La Bahía immediately, disregarding everything else. One, James Murphy, a colonist living in Refugio, was killed about a mile from the mission. Edward Perry, also from Refugio, was captured by Colonel Garay's men. Garay let Perry ride on to the mission, hoping that Ward would leave the church and proceed to Goliad via the La Bahía road where he could be easily trapped.

Ward did not fall for the scheme. He left all the Refugio colonists behind. He also left all the Mexican settlers that were there and all the wounded, including his own men. David Ayers, through whose efforts Fannin had been unwise enough to divide his forces, was left behind with Mrs. Ayers and her wounded brother. Two of Ward's men, named Wood and Simpson, volunteered to remain behind with the wounded.

During the late, dark night, Ward and his Georgia Battalion left the church to try to escape via the Copano road and to make their way east toward the Lavaca River. When Urrea and his men entered the church at dawn on March 15 he found six wounded men, four others, some colonist families, and several Mexicans who had been commandeered. All the Texan wounded, including Wood and Simpson, were shot and bayoneted. He ordered all his available cavalry to pursue Ward, but they could catch only some stragglers. His cavalry killed sixteen and took thirty-one prisoners.

Leaving Col. Rafael de la Vara and some men with instructions to keep a watch on the port of Copano, Urrea sent a detachment of cavalry ahead of him to intercept any communications with the enemy, and to observe his movements at short range. Then, with 200 men, infantry and cavalry, he left on the march to Goliad and was told that his advance cavalry had captured another fourteen of Ward's men.

Urrea had been disregarding orders from Santa Anna and the Mexican government that all Texan prisoners should be shot. Now he was hearing from some of his staff concerning this. In his diary of March 16 he wrote:

> The many hardships endured by my division and the rigor of the climate that was felt particularly by the troops accustomed to one more mild, made my position extremely difficult because of the necessity of properly guarding the adventurers that I had taken prisoners. I constantly heard complaints and I perceived the vexation of my troops. I received petitions from the officers asking me to comply with the orders of the general-in-chief and those of the supreme government regarding prisoners. These complaints were more loud on this day because, as our position was not improved, I found myself threatened from El Copano, Goliad, and Victoria. I was obliged to move with rapidity in order to save my division and destroy the forces that threatened us. Ward had escaped with 200 men; the

infantry was very poor and found itself much affected by the climate. I was unable, therefore, to carry out the good intentions dictated by my feeling, and I was overcome by the difficult circumstances that surrounded me. I authorized the execution, after my departure from camp, of thirty adventurers taken prisoners during the previous engagements, setting free those who were colonists or Mexicans.[5]

13

FANNIN MOVES AT LAST

On Sunday morning, March 13, the scouts Deaf Smith and twenty-four-year-old Capt. Henry Karnes arrived at Houston's camp in Gonzales with a party of four: Mrs. Susannah Dickinson, and her fifteen-month-old daughter, Angelina; Joe, Travis' black body servant; and Ben, the American black orderly of Santa Anna's aide, Colonel Almonte. Santa Anna had sent them on to Houston with news of the Alamo's fall. Mrs. Dickinson, wife of a captain of ordnance under Travis, confirmed that the Alamo had fallen and that the gallant Travis, Bowie, and Crockett, with all the other defenders, had perished. When they heard the news of the fall of the Alamo twenty of Houston's troops left him, and for the rest of his life he referred to them as deserters.

Shortly after Houston had digested the horrible news from Mrs. Dickinson, another scout reported in with information that General Ramirez y Sesma, accompanied by 600 infantry, 150 cavalry with light artillery and ammunition, was on the move toward Gonzales and should reach there by late that night or early the next morning. Houston now had around 400 men under his command. He decided, under the circumstances, not to go to San Antonio, but to fall back to Burnham's Crossing on the Colorado River, approximately fifty miles to the east. He gave orders to dump the artillery in the river and, followed by one ammunition wagon drawn by four oxen, the rag-tag army and a

95

horde of civilian followers began its retreat. Deaf Smith was left behind with a mounted rear guard to send along refugees.

The next day Sesma entered Gonzales only to see the town in flames and learn that Houston had fled in retreat. Once more he started pursuing his quarry.

Fannin, at his Fort Defiance, was still wondering what had happened to Ward and King. Dr. J. H. Barnard of his staff thought he was only awaiting their return to the fort before leaving it. The doctor certainly did not think Fannin disobeyed any orders from Houston to evacuate La Bahía and retreat to Victoria, as he made clear in his diary:

> . . . about this time, certainly before to-day, came in the order from Gen Houston to Col. Fannin to retreat to Victoria. This was the first and only communication had from Gen. Houston, while he was at Goliad. In fact, it was the first intimation we had of his whereabouts. The necessity of a retreat was now palpable to all. So far from Col. Fannin wishing to disobey the order, I know from his own lips that he intended to conform to it, as soon as the Georgia battalion should return; and I had heard him before this express a wish that Gen Houston would come on and take command of the troops. The alleged disobedience of Col. Fannin to Gen. Houston's order is an undeserved censure on a gallant soldier, and that he wrote back a refusal I know to be false. Circumstances enabled me to possess a positive knowledge on these points, and justice to both the dead and the living require of me thus to state it.[1]

Dr. Jack Shackelford, who served with Fannin as a captain, later made a statement that Houston's letter was received by Fannin on March 14. Fannin promptly sent a courier to Ward requesting him to immediately return to La Bahía. He also sent out parties, teams, and wagon carts, and commenced dismounting and hurtling several of his guns. The courier riding to Ward was intercepted by Urrea, who thus found out about Houston's orders and Fannin's plans.[2]

By March 16 Fannin had still received no word from Ward or King, and everyone was getting worried about what had happened to them. Capt. Hugh McDonald Frazer of the Refugio militia volunteered to go on to Refugio to see what happened to them, and promised to return within twenty-four hours. On March 17, Fannin ordered Colonel Horton and his cavalry to reconnoiter the enemy. By four o'clock that afternoon, Captain Frazer returned with his report on the happenings at Refugio and the capture and execution of King and his men. Then Horton and his men returned with the news that there was a large body of the enemy only a few miles from the fort, marching slowly and in good order. A council of war was held, and it was the unanimous opinion that they should abandon the fort the next day. Fannin ordered that a cannon they had buried be dug up and remounted. Also, fearful that an attack might be made that night, he doubled the guard.

Fannin and his men did not leave Fort Defiance on the eighteenth as planned. In the morning one of Urrea's cavalry patrols was sighted close to the fort. Colonel Horton and some of his scouts left the fort to confront them, but the enemy fled. Horton pursued them for a while and caught up with them; however, by now the Mexican patrol had reinforcements and it was their turn to chase Horton back to La Bahía.

As Horton and his men approached their sanctuary, all the rest of the horsemen in the fortress rode out to help him. The game of catch-me-if-you-can continued as the Mexicans, with the hot pursuit of the Texans, crossed the San Antonio River while the pursuers and the pursued fired sporadically at each other.

By now Urrea, who was close to Goliad, was joined by Col. Juan Morales with three cannon and 500 men.[3] He sent Morales and the picked companies from Jimenez and San Luis to go out and meet the Texans, and once more it was the Mexicans' turn to chase Horton. The latter managed to get to the old Mission Espiritu Santo, a few hundred yards from Fort Defiance near the river. At this point Captain Shackelford and his Red Rovers then went into action, assisted by the artillerymen. The latter mounted a gun on the wall and fired, but the distance was too great and the round fell short.

To assist Horton and his troops the artillery kept firing; the Red Rovers crossed the river and headed for the mission, but by the time they got there the Mexicans had withdrawn. Horton, Shackelford, and their men then went back to the nearby garrison of Fort Defiance.

The best part of the day had been spent, Horton's horses were tired from the day's activities, and the oxen in the fort had been left without food and water all day and were in no condition to haul the cannon and supplies. Evacuation of the fort was put off another day, so the men settled in for the night.

Urrea had established his camp three miles north of the fort to block any escape to Victoria, and had placed advanced cavalry pickets along the river to keep watch. Fannin for his part ordered another increase in the night sentries.

The night was cold and chilly due to a continual rain and a strong north wind, and men on both sides spent an uncomfortable night. Before daybreak of the nineteenth, Horton and his scouts went out on a reconnaissance. When they returned they reported the road was clear.

Finally, as Sam Houston had advised him to do so long ago, Fannin abandoned Fort Defiance and destroyed everything he could not take with him. Walls of the fortification ware torn down and all houses outside the walls were set on fire or otherwise destroyed. Large quantities of dried meat and the remaining corn and meal was piled up and burned.[4] Guns they were going to leave behind were spiked. Fannin wouldn't follow Houston's orders to destroy his cannon and he took nine of them along with him. Several wagon loads—including one with 500 spare muskets, which he refused to abandon, heavily laden with ammunition, baggage, and supplies—were taken along as they left the fort. Oddly, in their haste they forgot to take along any food.

Between nine and ten in the morning Fannin and his caravan slowly moved out of the fortress that had so long been their home, heading northeast toward Victoria about thirty-five miles away and slightly beyond the Guadalupe River. As the soldiers passed through the gates of the garrison, dark clouds of smoke from the smouldering flames that were consuming their provisions curled skyward.

Trouble began immediately. The cannon, baggage, and sick were drawn by Mexican oxen who did not understand the drivers' commands in English. When they left the fortress some became unmanageable and would not move forward, only backward, and it took the drivers some time to control the beasts.

More trouble began when they reached the San Antonio River, less than a mile away. According to Isaac D. Hamilton, who survived both the subsequent battle on the Plains of Coleto and the execution of the troops, one of the wagons broke down and a howitzer, which Fannin had insisted be brought along, bogged down. It took around two dozen men to manhandle that large bulk of brass across the ford.[5] At last the rear guard cleared the river and once more Fannin and his army were on their way to their appointment in Samarra. It was now around ten o'clock.

With the various wagons loaded with as much equipment and ammunition as they could possibly carry, and with too few horses and oxen to pull the carts with any degree of speed, it was determined that some wagons needed to be emptied of their contents. Eventually several wagons were broken up or simply abandoned until, according to Ehrenberg, "We kept only two wagons, our store of powder and the four artillery pieces; to these we harnessed all the horses and oxen."[6]

After slowly trudging some six or seven miles out and after crossing Manahuilla Creek and while still on the prairie, Fannin called a halt of about an hour so his oxen could graze and rest and his army relax. Shackelford and other officers protested, urging that the army move on to Coleto Creek, where there was water and also heavy woods which would furnish excellent protection in the event of an attack from the enemy. Fannin and some others had only contempt for the Mexicans and didn't believe they would follow the Texans. The protesters were overruled.

Shortly after the march resumed, another cart broke down and its load was transferred to another cart. Colonel Horton detailed guards for the flanks and rear of the column, and he and the rest of his cavalry advanced to reconnoiter the Coleto crossing. It was about three o'clock in the afternoon and some eight or nine miles from Goliad when Mexican cavalry appeared at the edge of the woods near Fannin's troops. Shackelford, in his later account of the affair, wrote:

> A few horsemen were seen off to the right, in the edge of the prairie, but they soon entered the timber again. Suddenly four of Horton's mounted scouts who had been detailed to guard the rear, came hurrying forward. In their contempt for the Mexicans they had dismounted and were lying down when they saw the Mexicans advance just in time to escape. Three of the scouts passed off to the right of the column and never halted until they had joined their troops in the Coleto woods. The fourth, Herman Ehrenberg, halted and joined the column. Soon a dark mass was seen

moving out from the Manahuilla woods, in the rear, which proved to be a column of dragoons. They deployed and came on at a gallop. As they approached, Colonel Fannin ordered some of the cannons to fire upon them, while yet marching, in an effort to reach the timber, only about a mile ahead. The shots fell short, and the enemy continued to move upon the right and front of the Texans so as to cut them off from the timber.[7]

During that morning Urrea's advance guards had turned in a report of no news. The general, thinking his foe was still in his fortress, was about to make an inspection of the area to see what the situation was when he received information that Fannin had left his garrison and was on the way to Victoria. He then put 360 infantry and 80 cavalry on notice to be prepared to march, and when his spies' reports turned out to be accurate, at eleven o'clock he set out to pursue Fannin. First, though, he left the rest of his force and the artillery and baggage under the command of Col. Francisco Garay with instructions to explore Fort Defiance and to occupy it if he found it to be abandoned.

After he was on the march about two miles, Urrea's advance scouts told him they had gotten close to Fannin and apparently he was not taking all of his Goliad force with him. Urrea then ordered 100 infantry to return to Goliad and to protect the artillery and ammunition that was being brought up. According to Urrea he caught up with Fannin about one-thirty in the afternoon in what he referred to as "the headland of Encinal del Perdido" or Oak Grove of the Perdido Creek. Fannin was still in the prairie about a mile from the woods.

When Fannin saw Urrea's troops, he immediately formed his men into a hollow square for better defense. In the front were placed the Red Rovers and the New Orleans Greys; in the rear Capt. Burr H. Duval's Mustangs; and on the other sides he placed the other troops. Urrea had no artillery with him but was expecting it momentarily, so he decided to engage Fannin at once. He ordered Col. Juan Morales to charge the left flank with his rifle companies. Urrea and two infantry companies attacked the right flank. Col. Mariano Salas covered the front, and the cavalry of Col. Gabriel Nunez covered the rear. The date was March 19, and it was General Urrea's thirty-ninth birthday.

The Battle of Coleto Plains then began.

14

THE BATTLE OF COLETO PLAINS

Fannin's decision to stop and rest his oxen and troops and not continue on to the safety of the woods was unwise and was to cost him dearly. When Urrea's cavalry had caught up with him and the battle commenced, Fannin was in a very poor position on the plains, being caught in an area that some estimated as being six to seven feet below its surroundings. He was unable to take advantage of an old military maxim that advises one to always take the high ground if possible. Consequently, his defensive maneuver in forming a square was a good one under the circumstances. The wagons were pulled up to form barricades, and the baggage was placed to form breastworks for his infantrymen. He placed his artillery at the corners of the square.

When the battle began Horton and his men were returning from their reconnaissance and had a full view of the engagement. One of his lieutenants, a man named Moore, objected to any attempt to reach Fannin's beleaguered troops by trying to penetrate the Mexican lines. He stated that it was impossible and they would all be cut to pieces. Then he dashed off in another direction, taking with him most of approximately thirty men. Horton, being left with so few men, also retired from the field and headed toward Victoria. Fannin was thus left with no cavalry to help him fight off the enemy. Captain Shackelford, who later heard the story from a couple of the men who were with Horton, stated he

didn't think that Horton, with all of his force, could have pene-
trated through the immense number of Mexican cavalry.[1]

At the commencement of the battle the enemy had no
artillery with them, so Urrea had to depend on his cavalry and
infantry alone. Later in his account of the engagement he wrote
in his diary:

> In order to obtain a quick victory, I ordered my troops to
> charge with their bayonets at the same time that Col. Morales
> did likewise on the opposite flank; and, according to previous
> instructions, the central column advanced in battle formation
> sustaining a steady fire in order to detract the attention of the
> enemy while we surprised the flanks. Though our soldiers
> showed resolution the enemy was likewise unflinching. Thus,
> without being intimidated by our impetuous charge, it
> maneuvered in order to meet it; and, assuming a hammer
> formation on the right, they quickly placed three pieces of
> artillery on this side pouring a deadly shower of shot upon
> my reduced column. A similar movement was executed on
> the left, while our front attack was met with the same courage
> and coolness. Our column was obliged to operate in guerril-
> las in order to avoid, as far as possible, the withering fire of
> the enemy, who kept up a most lively fire for each one of their
> soldiers had three and even four loaded guns which they
> could use at the most critical moment.[2]

The Mexican infantry on the right flank was the celebrated
Tampico regiment, and on the bare plains they had absolutely
no protection—no buildings or trees to hide behind; no cactus,
only the grass—and while standing to reload their British-made
rifles they were immediately felled by the accurate fire of the
Texan volunteers. Seeing this, Urrea ordered them to lie down
in the grass for whatever protection they could get and fire from
the ground. They seldom did it twice because whenever a
Mexican head rose to fire it was promptly drilled by a rifleman
to whom sharpshooting was second nature.

Dr. Barnard was one of those who thought Fannin should
not have made his rest stop but pushed on toward water and the
safety of the woods. He later wrote of the battle in his memoirs:

> . . . Colonel Fannin had committed a grievous error in suffering us to stop on the prairie at all. We ought to have moved on at all hazards and all costs until we reached the timber. We might have suffered soy7me loss but we could have moved on and kept them at bay as easily as we repulsed them while stationary.
>
> Fannin behaved with perfect coolness and self-possession throughout, and evinced no lack of bravery . . .[3]

When Urrea's cavalry under the command of Colonel Nunez charged from the rear of the square, they ran into a surprise. Fannin's Polish artillerymen, led by Capt. H. Francis Petrussewicz, let the cavalry draw near. Then the Texan front line opened up. The Mexicans were caught with a heavy barrage of artillery and were mowed down by grape and canister.

The battle continued with Urrea's cavalry attacking the flanks of Fannin, to be repulsed by artillery; then the Mexican infantry would advance once more, only to be thrown back.

Urrea, an old cavalryman, personally led a cavalry charge to Fannin's rear but was driven off repeatedly after several attempts, and was finally forced to retire "not without indignation," as he wrote in his diary. Other units of the Mexicans charged the Texans to no avail, as they were steadily driven back by the rifle fire and bayonets of the defenders. During the fighting, Fannin was wounded three times, once in the thigh.

The fighting became general, and Urrea decided to make a new and simultaneous charge on all fronts. Once more he placed himself at the head of his cavalry and led the charge on one of the fronts, while all his troops advanced to within fifty and even forty paces from the hollow square. The Texans redoubled their efforts and beat off the charges, and Urrea ordered his men to retreat.

As darkness was approaching, Campeachy Indians from Yucatan were brought in. Excellent sharpshooters, they hid in the tall grass about thirty yards from the Texan lines, from which they poured a destructive fire and did great damage.[4] Many of the Indians were killed by return fire; as soon as the flashes from their muskets were observed in the darkness, a deadly shot answered.

Among the wounded by the fire of the Indians was a young man named Harry Ripley. Eighteen years old, Ripley was the son of General Ripley of Louisiana. First he had his thigh broken. A Mrs. Cash, whose husband and fourteen-year-old son were with Fannin's troops, helped him into a cart and fixed a prop for him to lean on and a rest for his rifle. Ripley continued to fight until another shot broke his right arm and took him out of commission.

When night fell Urrea called off the battle as he was running low on ammunition. His expected reinforcements with additional men, provisions, and ammunition had gotten lost.[5] Both sides then rested and counted up their losses.

Although the artillery of the volunteers had done great damage, it had not been as effective as it should have been. With no water available the men hadn't been able to sponge the barrels after firing; consequently, the barrels got overheated and could not be used very rapidly. In addition, due to the low position they were in due to the depression of the ground, they could not be used to their best advantage as sometimes they would fire over the heads of the attackers. Also, virtually all the artillerymen had been killed and their places had been taken by infantrymen unfamiliar with cannon.

When the day's losses were totaled the Texans had seven men killed and sixty wounded, some of them mortally. Young Ehrenberg from Germany claimed in his memoirs that a little less than 750 Mexicans lay on the prairie at the end of the day's fighting, while Fannin had lost about one-fifth of his men.[6]

To make sure Fannin's troops did not attempt to get away during the night Urrea placed cavalry and infantry pickets at various places on the roads to Goliad and Victoria and another group between the two. During the night he closed the circle formed by his advance guards and moved his scouts forward until they could observe every movement of Fannin and his men.

Fannin had men digging a ditch around the square to form some breastworks. Behind it, the men heaped their wagons and the carcasses of dead horses and oxen to give them additional protection in case of attack.

The Texan volunteers spent a miserable cold night without food or water. Many, especially the wounded, suffered from thirst and a few of them, consumed by burning fever, begged pitifully for water, but all canteens were empty. In addition, there was not a breath of wind. The young men of Fannin's army who had come to Texas in a spirit of adventure, seeking excitement and so eager to see action, were now seeing the realities of war firsthand, and many of them didn't like it. Quite a few were grousing about Fannin stopping on the plains instead of not pressing on to the safety of the not-so-distant woods and water.

In his book *With Milam and Fannin in Texas*, Ehrenberg mentioned that the men now bitterly regretted all the hesitations and delays that had prevented them from taking shelter in the woods, where it would have been much more difficult for their adversary to have defeated or destroyed them. He remarked that the Greys wanted Fannin to make a bold dash at the Mexicans and force a passage through their army no matter how desperate the odds were, but Fannin pointed out that they couldn't possibly leave their badly wounded companions behind and they had no means to transport them.

Urrea was trying his best to keep the Texans' lives miserable. What oxen hadn't been killed by normal Mexican gunfire during the day had been deliberately shot by snipers on Urrea's orders. For harassment, during the night Urrea had his buglers constantly sound false bugle calls interspersed with frequent cries of "sentinel alert."

At daybreak, Sunday, March 20, Urrea issued orders for the Jiminez battalion to take its position in battle formation; the rifle companies were to advance along the open country and the cavalry in two wings was to charge both flanks. Once the troops were in position they were issued their rations, consisting of hardtack and roast meat, the beef being furnished by oxen of Fannin's army that had wandered outside the defensive square the day previously and been caught by the Mexicans.

At six-thirty in the morning Urrea's delayed reinforcements, weapons, and ammunition arrived. In his diary the general stated it consisted of 100 infantry, two four-pounders, and a howitzer. Urrea placed his new weapons protected by his rifle companies about 160 paces from the Texan breastworks. The rest of the infantry was formed in a column that was to advance to the left of his battery when it opened fire. According to

Shackelford, after a few artillery shots the Mexicans raised a white flag but it was soon taken down.

Dr. Barnard, in his account of the Battle of the Coleto Plains, gave his verdict of what happened on that Sunday morning. According to the doctor, Urrea's reinforcements consisted of three or four hundred men, 100 pack mules, two pieces of artillery, and ammunition, thus increasing the enemy force to at least 1,300, compared to about 200 men with Fannin, not including the wounded. Once more this brought on the question as to whether the Texans should surrender or make a desperate dash through the Mexican lines to the river. The Texans knew the faithlessness and barbarity of the Mexican troops by what had happened to Johnson, Grant and King, but a dash to the river was out of the question unless they abandoned their wounded to certain death, and that they could not do. To stand and fight, without provisions, water, and with very little ammunition would only postpone the inevitable.

There was also another factor to be considered. The breastworks thrown up the night before of wagons and dead carcasses would provide good protection against musketry but would be useless against the artillery that Urrea now had. As soon as Fannin saw Urrea's reinforcements arrive with artillery, he knew the fate of the engagement was determined. And he still had to listen to the piteous cries of his wounded as they begged for surrender so their parched throats would be given water. [7]

The officers conferred among themselves and then asked the men for their opinions. Barnard was in Captain Shackelford's company, and when the question was put to them, Barnard and his companions were of the opinion that if Urrea would agree to a formal capitulation and adhere to it, thus saving the Texan wounded, they should surrender. Otherwise, they would rather fight it out to the last man. Captain Shackelford resolutely declared that he would not agree to any alternate course that involved an abandonment of the wounded men. At first Fannin was opposed, saying, "We whipped them off yesterday, and we can do so again today." Then he inquired if the opinion of his men was unanimous, and when he found out that nearly all the men agreed with the decision, he ordered a white flag to be hoisted. [8]

Maj. B. C. Wallace, who was now Fannin's second-in-command since Ward and his battalion had left for Refugio, and Capt. Francis J. Desauque as interpreter, went out on the battlefield to meet the Mexican representatives, who were Col. Juan Morales, Col. Juan José Holsinger, and Urrea's aide, José de la luz Gonzales.

Now, at this distance, there seems to be a considerable difference in opinion as to the exact terms of surrender agreed upon by Urrea and the Texans. According to Urrea, Morales returned quickly, stating that Fannin wished to capitulate.

> My reply restricted itself to stating that I could not accept any terms except an unconditional surrender. Messrs. Morales and Salas proceeded to tell this to the commissioners of the enemy who had already come out from their trenches. Several communications passed between us; and, desirous of putting an end to the negotiations I went over to the enemy's camp and explained to their leader the impossibility in which I found myself of granting other terms than an unconditional surrender as proposed, in which of the fact I refused to subscribe to the capitulation submitted consisting of three articles. Addressing myself to Fannin and his companions in the presence of Messrs. Morales, Salas, Holzinger and others, I said conclusively "if you gentlemen wish to surrender at discretion the matter is ended, otherwise I shall return to my camp and renew the attack."[9]

Both Dr. Barnard and Capt. Jack Shackelford, who were in private life physicians, were emphatic in their disagreement with General Urrea's version of the surrender as it appears in his diary. According to Barnard, ". . . after some parley a capitulation with General Urrea was agreed upon, the terms of which were: that we should lay down our arms and surrender ourselves as prisoners of war. That we should be treated as such according to the usage of civilized nations. That our wounded men should be taken back to Goliad and properly attended to, and that all private property should be respected."

These were the terms that Colonel Fannin distinctly told his men, on his return, had been agreed upon, and such was confirmed by Major Wallace and Captain Desauque, the interpreter.

> We were told that articles of the capitulation were reduced
> to writing and signed by the commanders of both sides, and
> one or two of their principal officers; that the writings were
> in duplicate and each commander retained a copy. . . . We
> were also told though I cannot vouch for the authority that
> as soon as possible we should be sent to New Orleans under
> parole, not to serve any more against Mexico during the war
> in Texas: but it seemed to be confirmed by an observation
> of the Mexican Col. Hollbyinger [Holsinger] who was to
> superintend the receiving of our arms as we delivered them
> up, he exclaimed: "Well, gentlemen, in ten days, liberty and
> home."[10]

The recollection of Jack Shackelford in his notes is virtually
identical with that of Barnard. He states the first words Colonel
Holsinger uttered after a very polite bow were "Well, Gentlemen,
in eight days liberty and home." He says the terms of capitulation
were then written in both the English and Mexican languages,
and read two or three times by officers who could speak and read
both languages. The instruments which embodied the terms of
surrender were then signed and interchanged in the most formal
and solemn manner and were in substance as follows:

1. That we should be received and treated as prisoners-of-war,
   according to the usages of the most civilized nations.
2. That private property should be respected and restored that
   the side-arms of the officers should be given up.
3. That the men should be sent to Copano and thence to the
   United States in eight days or so soon thereafter as vessels
   could be procured to take them.
4. That the officers should be paroled and returned to the
   United States in like manner.

"I assert most positively that this capitulation was entered
into without which a surrender never would have been made."[11]

Shackelford later commented that he had read General
Urrea's pamphlet on the affair and remarked: ". . . On this
point, as well as his denial of any capitulation, I never read a
more villianous *falsehood* from the pen of any man who aspired
to the rank of general."[12]

Many years later, Eugene C. Barker, noted historian of the

University of Texas, in the Mexican archives found a copy of the terms of surrender, written in Spanish. An English translation of the document reads as follows:

> Surrender of the force at Goliad under the command of James W. Fannin.
>
> Article 1. The Mexican troops having placed their battery 160 paces from us and the fire having been renewed, we raised a white flag; Col. Jean Morales, Col. Mariano Salas and Lieut. Col. of Engineers Juan José Holzinger came immediately. We proposed to surrender at discretion, and they agreed.
>
> Article 2. The commandant, Fannin, and the wounded shall be treated with all possible consideration upon the surrender of all their arms.
>
> Article 3. The whole detachment shall be treated as prisoners of war and shall be subject to the disposition of the supreme government.
>
> Camp on the Coleto, between the Guadalupe and La Bahia, March 20, 1836.
>
> > B. C. Wallace, commandant
> > J. M. Chadwick, aide
> > Approved: James W. Fannin.

> Since, when the white flag was raised by the enemy, I made it known to their officer that I could not grant any other terms than an unconditional surrender, and they agreed to it through the officers expressed, those who subscribe the surrender have no right to any other terms. They have been informed of the fact, and they are agreed. I ought not, can not, nor wish to grant any other terms.
>
> > José Urrea
> > This is a copy, Mexico,
> > March 7, 1837.
> > Ignacio del Carral.

Later, in his diary, Brigadier General Urrea remarked:

> Had I been in a position to do so I would have at least guaranteed them their life. Fannin was a gentleman a man of courage a quality which makes us soldiers esteem each other mutually. His manners captivated my affection and if it had

been in my hand to save him together with his companions I would have gladly done so. All I could do was to offer him to use my influence with the general-in-chief which I did from the Guadalupe.

No English version of the surrender document has ever come to light, and as Pruett and Cole state in their *Goliad Massacre*, it is quite understandable why the English version has never surfaced, considering the events of the coming week.

15

In Captivity

Once the surrender papers were signed the men started packing their equipment and baggage, and Urrea, with most of his force, headed for Victoria. To be in command of the garrison of La Bahía in his absence, he appointed Col. José Nicolas de la Portilla.

Now that the hostilities were over, many Mexicans came into camp to wander over the field covered with debris, corpses, and carcasses of dead horses and oxen. They were intrigued by the nine pieces of artillery, three flags, 1,000 rifles, and many good pistols the Texans had surrendered. Suddenly, a light flashed through the misty morning, a dull report followed, and a terrible jarring of the air combined with it. The powder magazine had blown up, wounding about fifteen men, and killing a Texan named Johnson.

It was about two o'clock in the afternoon before the equipment and baggage were loaded onto the carts, and the prisoners, including the walking wounded and accompanied by about 200 Mexican guards, started slowly trudging back to Goliad. No provisions for food or water had been made for them, and the guards assigned to escort them showed no sympathy or concern for their discomfort. Finally, the prisoners reached the San Antonio River, and although they had to wade in the cold water, at least they got to relieve their raging thirst. Shortly afterward, they were back at the garrison they had left with such high hopes only a few hours previously.

As there had been no room on the carts for the seriously wounded, they had had to remain back at the battle site, under guard until carts could be sent back to pick them up. Dr. Barnard and Dr. Joseph E. Field, who had been in Texas for over two years, were left behind to care for the wounded, which included Fannin, Capt. Jack Shackelford of the Red Rovers, his son and nephew, and Captains Desauque, Samuel Overton Pettus, and Hugh McDonald Frazer. In addition, two or three uninjured volunteers were also delegated to stay behind and assist the wounded.

It took two days for enough wagons to get back to the Coleto Plains and take all the wounded back to Fort Defiance, and the last group of the wounded, including the doctors and other attendants, moved out on March 22. At Manahuilla Creek, the party met General Urrea with about 1,000 men, going to Victoria. A Mexican captain of the escort discovered that Desauque could speak excellent Spanish and engaged him in conversation and walked along with the Texans for several miles, according to Barnard. It was dark when the group reached the San Antonio River, and as it was three feet deep, they waded it. When the Mexican captain went back to oversee some wagons that had not yet crossed, according to Barnard in his memoirs:

> Captain Desauque now remarked in a very serious tone, that contrasted strangely with the cheerfull voice in which he had been conversing: "I am now prepared for any fate." The words, and his manner, struck us with surprise, and he was asked if he had ascertained by anything the captain had said that treachery was meditated. "No," he replied and ominously repeated his former remark. The idea struck me that here was a chance to escape by silently dropping into the water while the guards and their captain were on the other side and from the darkness could not see me; in two or three minutes I would have floated beyond their reach, and being a good swimmer, could then easily escape. I stopped to consider the matter more fully and directly the captain and his guard were alongside of us and thus by indecision in a critical moment lost the chance.[1]

When Barnard and the wounded—which included all the Mexican wounded as well as the Americans—arrived at La Bahía on Tuesday night, they were put in the church where all the prisoners were held. The wounded Americans were put on one side of the church, and the wounded Mexicans on the other side.[2]

The small church was already crowded with the first arrivals, and when the new group was added to their numbers, conditions became almost unbearable. The body heat of the men, plus the lack of air inside the building, made the temperature stifling. The church was so small and crowded that men had to sit back to back and none could stretch out. Those who slept, if at all, had to do it standing up.

Ehrenherg, who arrived the first day, reported that the guards refused the prisoners' entreaties for food and water, and it was not until eight o'clock of the twenty-second before six men were allowed to go to the river and bring back water for their thirsty comrades. They were still not given any food. Wednesday brought very little water and still no food. The prisoners started getting restless and demanding food, so finally the colonel in charge of the Tres Villas, the Mexican troops who guarded the men, came to see the Texans, accompanied by Colonel Holsinger. The colonel explained his own men had no rations either, but the Texans were positive he was lying. Finally, at six o'clock in the evening, the guards brought in a ration of about six ounces of raw meat per man. Without any way of cooking the meat, the men stripped the wall of their woodwork and soon two fires were burning to cook the meager rations.

The night was cold with a periodic light rain, and there were few blankets to go around, but at least the men had some space to move around or to lie down. Although the guards forbade the townspeople to sell the prisoners any food, it wasn't too long before a black market had developed with the Texans trading anything they had for food, and it wasn't too long until the Mexicans—both the townspeople and the guards—were in possession of clothing, blankets, money, and anything else of value the Texans had. Thievery by the Mexican guards was not uncommon. Ehrenherg later complained that a beautiful blanket of his was stolen.

Time passed slowly for the prisoners in their cramped quarters. The formerly lively and spirited youngsters had been away from home for about six months in their quest for adventure. Now they were lonely and homesick. Several of them had flutes among their personal possessions that hadn't been sold or stolen, and when they played "Home, Sweet Home," many of them wept openly.[3]

The Mexicans had stripped the Texans of virtually all articles they had—even their pocketknives. Dr. Barnard's medical instruments were stolen, as were Shackelford's clothes. On Wednesday Barnard spoke to Fannin and asked him to address a note to the Mexican commander requesting medical instruments to replace his stolen ones, as he needed them to treat not only the Americans but to treat the wounded Mexicans as well. Nothing was done except that all the wounded were removed from the church and placed on the west side of the fort, under guard of a company of infantry.

On Thursday, March 24, Mexican officials approached the four American physicians, Doctors Barnard, Shackelford, Field, and Hale, and politely asked them, as a favor, to attend to the Mexican wounded, as they had no physicians of their own. The Texans, not to be outdone in politeness, replied that they would he glad to do so. The Mexicans, however, made it clearly understood that the Mexican wounded had to be taken care of first. The Americans protested but to no avail. Finally, a Mexican surgeon arrived, but didn't give the Americans any assistance. It took nearly the whole day for the American doctors to tend to the Mexicans before they could give their own men any attention. Then they had so little time they could only dress some of the severest wounds and leave the rest altogether; some of the injured at this time had received no treatment at all since the battle began.

It was on this day that Maj. William C. Miller and eighty men arrived in camp. From Nashville, Tennessee, Major Miller and his men had landed at Copano Bay on March 17 to join the Texan cause. Before they had even had time to unload their arms and ammunition from their ship, they had been immediately surrounded by the forces of Col. D. N. Bara and told of Fannin's surrender. With Bara's assurances that they would be treated with all consideration if they surrendered to him, they did so. In spite of Bara's promise, they had been held at Copano, tightly bound and without food, for several days until Francita Alavez, wife of a Mexican officer, interceded for them and persuaded their captors to loosen their binds and give them a little food.

Once with Fannin and his troops in the congested garrison, Miller and some of his men volunteered their services as medical aides and were a great help to the Texan medical doctors.

The next day, the twenty-fifth, Colonel Ward and the survivors of his men who had escaped from Refugio were brought in to join the Texas prisoners.

When Ward and his men had left Refugio they marched through the woods and swamps where the enemy's cavalry could not follow until they reached the San Antonio River. On the second day of the retreat a few of Ward's men left the group and never rejoined it. The evening of the nineteenth Ward and his men heard the firing between Fannin and Urrea, judging it to be about ten miles away. They tried to reach the combat, but when darkness came they were in the Guadalupe swamp and spent the night there. The next day as they emerged from the swamp onto the prairie they were attacked by some Mexican cavalry. They fired three or four rounds and, with their powder being exhausted, once more retreated into the swamp and spent another night there. The next day, the twenty-first, they set out again for Victoria and were captured by Urrea's troops, who were also heading for Victoria. That morning, Capt. Rafael Pretalia of the Cuautla Regiment had captured seven of Ward's stragglers headed for Victoria and had promptly executed them.

Ward, Maj. Warren J. Mitchell, and Capt. Isaac Ticknor then conferred with Urrea and reported back to their troops with the information Urrea had offered the same terms he had offered Fannin. If they surrendered they would be marched to Copano and either sent from there to New Orleans, held as prisoners of war, or would be exchanged.

According to Urrea, his forces had captured four of the Americans, who had come out of the woods looking for food, and had sent one of the prisoners back to Ward with instructions that if they did not surrender immediately at discretion they would all perish shortly. Ward then solicited an interview with the general. Five minutes of conversation was sufficient for him to agree to surrender the 100 men under his command, among whom were ten officers.

Lieutenant Colonel Ward didn't trust Urrea. When he later reported back to his forces, he said the Mexicans were the same people they had beaten off at Refugio, only there were not so many of them. (In his diary, Urrea claimed he had 200 men on foot and fifty cavalry.) Ward believed if they could hold off any attack until nightfall they could evade the Mexicans and get out of their dangerous position. He believed they were confronted by a faithless enemy and faithless surrender. He also believed, regardless of the terms offered, surrender would only result in their being butchered later. It was their best hope to resist; in that way, some of them might live.

When a vote of the group was taken, the majority wanted to accept the terms given and surrender. They came out of the woods, turned over their ammunition to Urrea's troops, and were marched back to Goliad.

On the evening of March 26 the long arm of Santa Anna struck the garrison of La Bahía. An express courier from *el presidente* brought to Colonel Portilla, the commandant at La Bahía, an order, a copy of which had been forwarded to General Urrea. The order was from Santa Anna, and its contents boded no good for the Texan prisoners:

> By a communication made to me by Colonel D. F. Garay, of that place, I am informed that there have been sent to you by General Urred, *two hundred and thirty four prisoners*, taken in the action of *Encinal del Perdido*, on the 19th and 20th of the present month; and as the supreme government has ordered that all foreigners taken with arms in their hands, making war upon the nation, shall be treated as pirates, I have been surprised that the circular of the said supreme government has not been fully complied with in this particular. *I therefore order, that you should give immediate effect to the said ordinance in respect to all those foreigners* who have yielded to the force of arms, having had the audacity to come and insult the republic, to devastate with fire and sword, as has

been the case in Goliad, causing vast detriment to our citizens; in a word, shedding the precious blood of Mexican citizens, whose only crime has been their fidelity to their country. I trust that, in *reply* to this, you will inform me that public *vengeance has been satisfied* by the punishment of such detestable delinquents. I transcribe the said decree of the government for your guidance, and that you may strictly fulfil the same, in the zealous hope that in the future, the provisions of the supreme government may not, for a moment, be infringed.

Headquarters, Bejar, March 23, 1836
Antonio López de Santa Anna[4]

Almost immediately, Colonel Portilla answered Santa Anna's order, telling his superior that at four o'clock the next morning the prisoners would be shot. However, he was in doubt as to what to do with Major Miller and his men, who had been captured at Copano. He passed the buck and asked the president what he should do in their case.

At eight o'clock of the same evening, Portilla received a communication from Urrea by special messenger. Among other things, Urrea said: "Treat the prisoners well, especially Fannin. Keep them busy rebuilding the town and erecting a fort. Feed them with the cattle you will receive from Refugio."[5]

At the headquarters of the Mexican president in San Antonio, Capt. D. N. Savariego received Portilla's letter plus a note from Portilla asking him to intervene with Santa Anna for clemency for Major Miller and his men who, he stated, had surrendered without making use of their arms, and had never engaged in battle against the Mexicans. Ramon Martínez Cara was secretary to Santa Anna. In his later account of the incident he took Savariego into Santa Anna's office and was present at the interview between the president and his subordinate. Hardly had Savariego presented Portilla's request for clemency than Santa Anna let out such a tirade demanding that the unfortunates from Copano be executed also, that the captain left the room in disgust. Shortly afterward, Santa Anna ordered a thorough investigation be made of the circumstances of Miller's surrender, and subsequently ordered that the Tennessean and his men be spared from the execution.[6]

In his diary for Saturday, March 26, Dr. Barnard reported that Fannin and Major Chadwick, his adjudant, returned that day from Copano. The two officers were given quarters in a small room in the church in a wing of Fort Defiance that was occupied by the surgeons and their assistants. "Rather crowded, to be sure," Barnard wrote, "but we had become accustomed to that." Fannin and Chadwick were in good spirits and endeavored to cheer up their new roommates. They spoke of the kindness with which they had been treated by Colonel Holsinger, who had gone to Copano, and their hopes of an early release. Fannin asked Barnard to dress his wounds, and spoke fondly of his wife and children, and at the end of the evening he had succeeded in raising Barnard's spirits.

16

TREACHERY AND EXECUTION

When Palm Sunday, March 27, 1836, arrived, the weather was hot and sultry, with gray clouds hanging over the horizon. During the night the artillery pieces which had been covering the fort's gate were moved to command the prisoners' camp, and Portilla's gunners stood by their weapons prepared to open fire if ordered. Several companies of the guards had been ordered into parade uniform and formed to face the prisoners.

Word had been passed to the prisoners that a ship was available at Copano Bay where they could board for New Orleans. Some were told to pack their belongings as they would leave immediately to embark. Others were to be sent on working parties while they were awaiting their time to depart.

At daylight Col. Francisco Garay went to the quarters of Doctors Shackelford and Barnard. Dr. Field, who roomed with them, at the moment was outside the fort. Garay took the two medical men to the gate of the fort where Major Miller and his Tennesseans were. Garay, who spoke excellent English, then told all the Americans to go to his quarters, which were in a peach orchard some three or four hundred yards from the fort, to wait for him. Miller and his men led the way with the doctors following. The doctors supposed they were being called upon to attend to some of the Mexican wounded. Arriving at Garay's quarters, Shackelford and Barnard were instructed to go into a

119

tent where they saw two men lying on the ground, completely covered up so their faces couldn't be seen. The two physicians naturally assumed those were to be their patients.

An English-speaking Mexican lad named Martínez came in and told them his orders were that they were to wait there until Garay returned. Soon the two men heard the volley of guns, and shouts and yells coming from the fort. Looking through some openings in the tent, Shackelford and Barnard could see several prisoners running at top speed with soldiers chasing them.

Colonel Garay finally returned to the tent and with a serious expression on his face remarked, "Keep still gentlemen, you are safe." He then told them of Santa Anna's order to execute everyone but said he had taken it upon himself to save the surgeons and about a dozen others under the plea that they had been taken without arms. While the doctors were in the tent they heard at least four distinct volleys being fired in as many directions and then irregular firing which continued an hour or two before it ceased.[1] Shackelford, commander of the Red Rovers, was particularly disturbed as among the group he had led from Alabama were his son and two nephews.

Later on the physicians found out exactly what happened. The prisoners were lined up in three groups, each with their own guards. The Greys were marched off toward the lower ford across the San Antonio River, heading toward the Victoria road. Another group was headed toward the Bexar road, while the detachment that contained Captain Shackelford's Red Rovers were headed down the Refugio road.

One group was under the command of the first adjutant, Augustin Alcerrica; the second group was commanded by Capt. Luis Balderas; while the third was under the orders of Capt. Antonio Ramirez.

All of the sections were told different stories: they were going to gather up wood; they were going to proceed to Copano; or they were going to drive up beeves. No one suspected anything out of the ordinary until they suddenly found guns at their breasts and the firing started, point blank, at them. When they realized what was happening some of the troops yelled out to their comrades to die like men, while others, waving their hats, cried out "Hurrah for Texas!" Some of the more quick-witted, when they heard the first shots and realized what was happening, started running in the direction of the nearby woods and the San Antonio River and managed to escape. Many of them, however, were shot and bayoneted before they reached the woods or river. Of those fortunate enough to escape and avoid their execution, many of them eventually joined up with Gen. Sam Houston and his army at Gonzales.

Ehrenherg, the young German lad, was with the Greys. In his memoirs he mentions how the Greys started getting suspicious when, instead of the road they thought they were to take, found themselves taking the Victoria road. Their anxiety was furthered when then noticed how solemn the guards were. As a rule the guards were very talkative, but now they were silent. For the first time Ehrenherg noticed the guards were dressed in their parade uniforms, and their lack of baggage, and suddenly found himself thinking of the treachery of the Mexicans at Tampico, San Patricio, and the Alamo.

The officer in the lead quickly turned to the left off the main road and headed toward the San Antonio River. Nearby on the banks stood a row of mesquite trees five or six feet high. When the Texans were ordered to stop, the leader of the Mexicans ordered everyone to kneel, but the few Texans who understood the order didn't obey the command. Once more the commander ordered everyone to kneel and then his troops started firing. Ehrenberg heard volleys from where the other groups of Texans were, and as thick clouds of smoke rolled toward the river he ran for the river and jumped in after fighting off a Mexican who tried to shoot him.[2]

After Ehrenberg pulled himself out of the river he discarded everything he didn't need except his clothes. He wandered around the prairie for several days, living off the land. He couldn't find any water and eventually developed a severe headache and then a raging fever. Finally, the rains came and, clapping his hands and catching what he could, he drank thirstily. The rains helped settle his fever and his strength improved. After five or six days he came to a small settlement of eight or ten plantations and entered one. All the owners had long gone to join Sam Houston as members of the "Runaway Scrape." Unable to make a fire, Ehrenberg ate a dozen raw eggs and pushed on.

The following night he saw some Mexican troops but escaped into the darkness before they saw him. Still pushing on, he came to another deserted house. Finding cold food on the table in the empty house, he ate a huge dinner. The next day he saw a Mexican camp and decided to go boldly into it, posing as an American traveler who had lost his way. To his astonishment he discovered the camp was Urrea's headquarters, and there he ran into Colonel Holsinger, the German engineering officer. Holsinger failed to recognize him, but he and Urrea were suspicious of him and confronted him with some other Texan prisoners. Warned by a wink from Ehrenberg, the prisoners swore they had never seen him before and Urrea did not press the matter.

Urrea then took his troops to the Colorado River and followed it to Matagorda, where he dropped Holsinger off with a garrison of 400 men to build a fort while he went on to the Brazos to try to catch Houston. Ehrenberg stayed with Holsinger, who directed him and the other Texas prisoners to build a boat about twenty feet long.

Then, on April 24, news came in of Santa Anna's defeat at San Jacinto. Holsinger ordered his troops to march back to Mexico, and embarked with eight Mexicans and six Texans including Ehrenberg, in the boat they had built, together with a fourteen-foot, flat-bottomed scow they had found in the bay. For several days the small flotilla wandered about between a long island and the mainland, camping each night on the shore. One night Ehrenberg and a fellow Texan prisoner named John Adams walked away from the campfire and escaped. Eventually the two men ran across two more escapees, so the four turned back to Matagorda, which was now held by Texas troops. A delegation was sent out and quickly found Holsinger and his party. They took them back to Matagorda, where many of the angry Texans threatened to lynch them, but were dissuaded by Ehrenberg and Adams.

On June 1, 1836, Ehrenberg asked for and received an honorable discharge from Secretary of War Mirabeau B. Lamar.[3]

John Crittenden Duval, a member of his brother Burr's company, was one of the fortunate ones who escaped. Duval was a member of the largest division of men (comprising about 150) that was marched out of the garrison. As his detachment filed through the streets of Goliad, he heard several of the Mexican women exclaim "*pobrecitos*" (poor fellows), but the remarks made no impression on him.

After a march of about one-half mile from Goliad, a halt was ordered and the file of Mexican soldiers on his right counter-marched and formed behind the file on the opposite side. He and his companions still didn't suspect foul play until finally one of his friends shouted: "Boys, they are going to shoot us." At the same time he heard the clicking of the musket locks and the Mexicans fired, killing nearly every man in the front rank of the detachment.

Duval was lucky. He was in the rear rank. When he gathered his wits he dashed for the river, only to be accosted by a Mexican whose gun was empty. The Mexican charged, thrusting out his bayonet, but once more Duval's lucky star intervened. One of his friends, who was also dashing for the river, happened to run between Duval and his enemy and received the bayonet thrust in his chest. Duval then ran toward the river, and although he was shot at several times was unharmed and jumped into the river.

After swimming downstream a couple of hundred yards, Duval came to a shallow spot and climbed onto the ground. Shortly afterwards he ran across Samuel T. Brown, a member of the Georgia Battalion and a nephew of Lieutenant Colonel Ward. Then the two of them ran across John Holliday, a member of Duval's company, and the three of them headed for the Guadalupe River and for five days lived off of wild onions. They discovered a nest of young pigs and feasted for several days. After wandering for several days at random in the open country, they were taken prisoner by two Mexicans armed with guns and swords. But once more Duval managed to escape.[4]

Isaac D. Hamilton was a member of Dr. Jack Shackelford's Red Rovers. When his company was stopped and he saw the Mexican guards level their muskets, he noticed a brush fence nearby that had a low spot in it. When the guards fired, he was struck in the left thigh by a ball. He managed to keep on his feet and started running as best he could toward the low spot in the fence. He was in the process of jumping it when he was bayoneted in his right thigh. Disregarding his wounds he staggered toward some very high prairie grass, where he managed to hide until the Mexicans finally gave up their slaughter.

Due to the stiffness caused by his wounds, Hamilton found it impossible to walk, but was discovered by three of his friends who had also managed to escape the gunfire due to the smoke and the confusion. His three comrades shoulder-carried him for several days before, after the urging of one of the men, and with Hamilton's consent, they left him on his own.

Hamilton headed for the coast. He was in delirium much of the time, his wounds were infected, and his progress was very slow. He, like others, subsisted on wild onions, elm buds, and grass, along with a single dove he managed to kill with a stick. Eventually, he managed to reach a small town from which Urrea's troops had just departed. There he lived off the remains of some slaughtered beeves and a fish he had caught. He then found a hidden canoe and proceeded to the coast. Finally, he was recaptured by the Mexicans. It was fortunate that he next encountered Francita Alavez, whose husband, Telesforo Alavez, was a cavalry captain in the Mexican army and was presently in charge of the garrison at Victoria. Reuben Brown, a member of the ill-fated Dr. James Grant party that had been defeated at Agua Dulce Creek, had been scheduled for execution. Señora Alavez and a priest had used their influence to have his life spared. The good Señora had previously intervened on behalf of Maj. William Miller and his men when they landed at Copano Bay. Now Señora Alavez saved Hamilton from torture and execution by her intervention. Hamilton was then placed in hard labor until the defeat of Santa Anna became known, and Señora Alavez came to his rescue again by aiding him in an escape from the vengeful Mexican troops.[5]

Col. James Wood landed at Copano with Major Miller and was one of those taken prisoner. He later gave an interview to the *Louisville Journal* and related the scene from his vantage point in the peach orchard where he had been. Wood saw about fifty men make a break and run toward the bank of the San Antonio River, pursued by the infuriated infantry who overtook and killed many of them. About twenty-five of the Texans managed to jump into the river, but most were picked off by gunfire while in the water. Many of those who managed to get across the river to hide in the bushes or trees were hunted down and killed by Mexican cavalry who had been stationed across the river for just that purpose.[6]

All of the wounded lying in the hospitals were dragged into the fort and shot. Joseph H. Spohn of the Red Rovers was spared by Portilla as he spoke Spanish and was useful as an interpreter. After his release at the end of the war his story of the events of Palm Sunday were published by the New York *Evening Star* in the summer of 1836. Used as an interpreter by Portilla to tell Fannin he was going to be shot, Spohn was also a witness to Fannin's execution. As recounted by Spohn in the *Evening Star*, Fannin was the last of the Texans to be executed. The Mexicans had Spohn interpret for them to inform Fannin of his fate. Fannin took the news very calmly, and with no visible expression on his face, firmly walked to the place pointed out by the Mexican captain in charge of the firing squad. Spohn was then required to interpret the following sentence: "That for having come with an armed band to commit depredations and revolutionize Texas, the Mexican Government were about to chastise him."

Fannin gave the officer in charge his gold watch, a small beaded purse containing some doubloons, a part of a silk handkerchief, and a piece of canvas containing a double handful of dollars. He requested of the captain that he be shot in the breast, and said that he could keep the watch if he would make sure Fannin was given a decent burial. All of his last requests were ignored. He was shot in the head after being made to sit in a chair and have his hands bound. Then, with all of the other executed prisoners, his body was placed in a pile between alternate layers of wood and burned.[7]

All of the four doctors were spared, together with some hospital attendants and Major Miller and his men, who were used in various capacities. A couple of carpenters named White and Rosenbury also escaped execution. They were the ones hidden under the blanket when Shackelford and Barnard had entered their tent. The previous night, the carpenters had done some work for Colonel Garay that pleased him so much he had risked his life to save them by hiding them.

Among the troops from Colonel Ward's "Georgia Rattlers" battalion captured at Victoria were a number of carpenters. Colonel Holsinger, claiming that the Mexicans were of no value at heavy work, spared the lives of the carpenters as he indicated he needed them in getting the artillery over the river, and put some of them to work building boats. The fortunate carpenters were never sent back to Goliad and thus escaped execution.

On the day of the execution Francita Alavez arrived in Goliad, and when Fannin's men were being marched out to be massacred, she secreted several of the younger men in her quarters until after the killings and later helped them to escape. As Holsinger was marching a group of the prisoners out to the carnage, Alavez saw among the doomed men Benjamin F. Hughes, from Kentucky, a young boy of about fifteen. She begged Holsinger that he be released to her care, and the colonel graciously acceded to her request.[8]

Dr. Barnard kept a journal of his experiences in Texas and it was later published under the editorship of Hobart Huson. In the journal he relates a few days after the execution of the prisoners, Dr. Shackelford met Alavez. When she learned that his young son had been among those killed, she exclaimed: "Oh, why did I not know you had a son there? I would have saved him at all hazards."

Later on, for her humanitarian efforts among Texas prisoners at Victoria, Coleto, and Goliad, Señora Alavez acquired the name of "The Angel of Goliad."

Dr. Joseph E. Field was one of the four physicians spared from execution. For several weeks afterwards, his duty was to take care of injured and wounded Mexican officers. By giving good attention to their wounds he managed to gain their confidence. He did this to such a degree that a couple of the officers spoke to him several times about going to Mexico with them and living not as a prisoner, but as a friend.

Determined to escape at the first opportunity, Dr. Field and a fellow prisoner named Voss secured permission to sleep outside the fort. One night when it was very dark they went to the river pretending to go for water. They walked up the San

Antonio River about a mile until they came to a place that was fordable and crossed over, heading northward. Eventually, they crossed the Guadalupe and then the Colorado, and on the eleventh day, having traveled about 150 miles, they ran across a soldier who told them of Santa Anna's defeat and capture at the Battle of San Jacinto.

Continuing their journey the two men arrived at Velasco, which at that time was the seat of the new government. Field, whose health was very much impaired, obtained a furlough with permission to visit his family and friends in the United States.

After the massacre, Doctors Barnard and Shackelford went back to attending the wounded Mexicans. They were told that they would no longer be confined to the garrison but were at liberty to move around at large. Major Miller and his men, after giving their parole that they would not attempt to escape, were given the same privilege.

After about three weeks, at the request of Colonel Ugartechea, who had recently been appointed commandant of Goliad, Barnard and Shackelford took the wounded Mexican officers to San Antonio. In his diary Barnard later related how he and Shackelford looked at each other and noticed that both not only looked about ten years older, but felt the same way.[9]

Arriving at the Alamo the two doctors reported to Gen. Juan José Andrade, the commandant who read various letters written to him by Ugartechea. He then informed the two men that they were not to be considered as prisoners, but were entitled to their release and would be given their passports as soon as the wounded Mexican officers could get along without their medical services. He and Shackelford were also told that they had the freedom of the town.

Barnard later commented in his diary that various Mexican surgeons told him that after the Battle of the Alamo, over 400 wounded Mexicans were brought into the hospital. He thought more than that had been wounded, as he saw around 200 men with disabling injuries around town, and was told by various citizens that three or four hundred had died of their wounds.

On May 6 the city received the news of the defeat and capture of Santa Anna and that an armistice had been agreed upon. In the latter part of May, when the Mexican troops started leaving San Antonio, Barnard and Shackelford headed back to Goliad and met the advance guard of the Texas army now under the command of Gen. Thomas Jefferson Rusk of Georgia.

When General Filisola, in accordance with instructions from Santa Anna, was taking his defeated troops back to Mexico he was escorted by General Rusk. Rusk established his headquarters at Victoria but pushed on to Goliad to see that Filisola did not stop there, and arrived around the first of June. At the garrison of La Bahía, which Fannin had so enthusiastically renamed Fort Defiance some months before, he found the ghastly remains of the massacred Fannin and those under his command. Never having been given a decent burial, they were in partially covered trenches where their bodies had been dumped and burned. Many bones, gnawed by coyotes and dogs, were still on top of the ground.

Rusk promptly gave orders that on the morning of June 4, 1836, a formal military funeral would be conducted and that the remains of the soldiers would be given a decent burial.

Now Fannin and his men, who had passed into history, could rest in peace.

17

THE FINAL TALLY

In the July 1937 issue of the *Southwestern Historical Quarterly*, Vol. 43, No. 1, in an article entitled "The Men of Goliad," Harbert Davenport gave a list of those men under Fannin's command who perished during the Texas Revolution. There were 137 names of those who died. The discrepancy between the list of 342 names on the monument at Coleto Plains and Davenport's list is accounted for because Davenport included members of various units under Fannin who were killed or taken prisoner in various miltary actions, and were not killed during the Coleto Plains battle.

ROLL OF THOSE LOST OF COLONEL FANNIN'S COMMAND

1. Men of Colonel Francis Johnson's party surprised at and near San Patricio, February 27, 1836.

(a) Killed:

Coney, Henry	Hort, Dr. William M. W.
Dale, Benjamin	Pearson, Thomas K.
Bunsen, Dr. Gustav	Williams, William

Also, two San Antonio Mexicans in the service of Texas, whose names are not known.

(b) Captured and sent as prisoners to Matamoros:

Benson, William B.	Mahan, Phineas Jenks
Bryan, John	McKneely, Samuel W.
Copeland, George	Mitchell, Thomas S.
Francois, Sebastian	Pittman, Hutchins M.
Hall, William L.	Robison, Thomas
Kerr, Lucius H.	Spiess, John
Langenheim, William	

Also, five San Antonio Mexicans in the service of Texas, including Arreola and Sambrano, members of well-known families of Bexar. The Mexican archives should contain a list of these men.

(c) Escaped:

Beck, John F.	Love, John H.
Hufty, Edward H.	Miller, James M.
Johnson, Francis W.	Toler, Daniel J.

Beck, Miller, and Hufty were killed at Goliad with Colonel Fannin's men.

Colonel Johnson's party numbered 34 men. Two other Americans, whose names were unknown, were probably killed at San Patricio.

2. Men of Dr. James Grant's Party destroyed at Agua Dulce March 2, 1836.

(a) Killed:

Cass, James M.	Johnson, Joseph Smith
Carpenter, Joseph	Lewellen, Thomas
Denison, Stephen	Marshall, Horace Ovid
Grant, Dr. James	McLanglin, John C.
Heartt, Dr. Charles P.	Morris, Robert C.
Howard, J. T.	Wentworth, J. W.

(b) Captured and taken to Matamoros as prisoners:

Brown, Reuben R.	Curtis, Stillman S.
Collett, John	Jones, Nelson

Besides two Mexicans (one called "Cayetano"), whose full names can doubtless be found in the Mexican archives.

(c) Escaped:

Benavides, Placido	Moses, David

DeSpain, Randolph   Reed, James
Gatlin, William James   Scurlock, William

Those who escaped, except Benavides, joined Colonel Fannin
and were killed on March 27, save Scurlock, who was spared as a
nurse. Two unnamed Americans were killed at Agua Dulce;
Grant's party consisting of twenty-three Americans and three
Mexicans.

3. Men lost at and near Refugio in the fighting of March 14-16,
   1836, under Colonel Ward and Captain King.

<u>(a) Killed:</u>

Anderson, Samuel	Murphy, James
Armstrong, William S.	Ray, Anderson
Callison, James Henry	Rodgers, John B.
Colgrove, John H.	Sayle, Antoine
Cook, Thomas	Shelton, William
Davids, Fields	Simpson, William K.
Davids, Jackson	Smith, Gavin H.
Henley, James	Smith, Oliver
Heth, Joel P.	Stewart, John C.
Johnson, William R.	Toler, Robert A.
King, Amon Butler	Wallace, William
Kirk, Harvey H.	Weeks, Thomas G.
Ledbetter, Sneed	Winters, Christopher
Murphy, James B.	Wood, Samuel

This roll of names differs from that engraved on the Texas
Centennial monument at Refugio, in that it omits six names:

Brady, Leslie G. H.	Humphries, Jesse C.
Eadock, Henry H.	Penny, George W.
Gibbs, Lewis C.	Ward, John

contained on the monument roll, and adds four names:

Ray, Anderson	Wallace, William
Smith, Oliver	Weeks, Thomas G.

<u>(b) Captured with Captain King but not killed:</u>

Ayers, Lewis	Jenson, Charles
Dietrich, Francis	Odlum, Benjamin D.

Fagan, Nicholas   Osborn, Abraham H.

These were all spared by General Urrea, as colonists, except Jenson, or Johnson (Ehrenberg calls him a "Hamburger named Gensen") saved by Colonel Holsinger. John James of Refugio, captured at this time, was spared for the time being but was killed at Goliad with Colonel Fannin's men.

4. Men lost of whom escaped at and near Victoria during Colonel Ward's retreat.

(a) Water party sent forward by Colonel Ward March 16, 1836:

Butler, William H.	Hudson, Henry G.
Bright, John	Rogers, Hugh
Davis, O. H. Perry	Rutledge, Richard
Holt, David I.	

(b) Killed in action March 21, 1836:

Wilson, Joseph L.

(c) Killed as prisoners near Victoria, March 21, 1836:

Brooks, Daniel B.	Quirk, Thomas
Conner, Stith	

(d) Left Colonel Ward's command for Guadalupe on night of March 21 and escaped:

Andrews, Joseph	Moses, McK.
Bradford, Benjamin F.	Pease, L. T.
Hardaway, Samuel G.	Rains Joel D.
Heck, Charles Frederick	Rounds, George
Ingram, Allen	Trezevant, James P.

(e) Detailed to build boats at Victoria March 23, 1836, and subsequently escaped:

Barnwell, James H.	Lamkin, John James
Callaghan, James H.	Neely, James H.
Callahan, James H.	O'Daniel, John, Jr.
Gamble, Joseph	Patterson, Edward
Hammock, Roderick Pierce	Smith, Thomas J.
Hitchcock, Andrew Jackson	Spiller, John T.
Horry, Thomas	Stewart, Thomas G.
Kennymore, John C. P.	Wilkinson, William L.

All of those who knew A. J. Hitchcock in his old age are convinced that he escaped from the massacre on March 27, instead of having been detained at Victoria on the 23rd, but all existing official records and statements of contemporaries are in accord in listing him as one of the Victoria men.

(f) Detained at Victoria by General Urrea, afterward escaped:

Durain, Emanuel
Greene, Sion Duff
Moran, Martin
Mordecai, Benjamin
Welsh, William

5. Men of Colonel Fannin's Command, as of March 18-19, 1836.

(a) Escaped to Victoria, night of March 18:

Durret, Silas M.
Ludington, Elam

(b) Mounted men under Captain Horton,
not captured on March 19-20, 1836:

Adams, Thomas Jefferson
Austin, Norman
Baylor, Dr. John Walker
Betts, Jacob
Boom, Garrett E.
Bridgeman, George J.
Brooks, George Whitfield
Buckner, J. W.
Cantwell, Thomas
Clements, Joseph
DeMoss, Lewis
DeMoss, William
Eastland, Nicholas M.
Fenner, Joseph
Francis, William C.
George, Jefferson
Horton, Albert C.
Jones, Francis
Jones, John
Kincheloe, Augustus S.
Moore, James W.
Morgan, Charles
Osborn, John L.
Osborn, Thomas
Riley, Michael
Robinson, George N.
Scott, Levi Pendleton
Terrell, Christopher
Thompson, Thomas
Wheelwright, George W.
Wright, Ralph

(c) Killed in action or mortally wounded, March 19, 1836:

Dorsey, Alfred
Eigenauer, Conrad
Jackson, John
Kelly, John
Mann, William H.
McKnight, George
Petrussewicz, H. Francis
Quinn, William
Savage, William F.
Swords, Archibald

(d) Executed by order of General Santa Anna at Goliad, March 27, 1836:

Abercrombie, Wiley A.
Adams, James Moss
Aldridge, Isaac
Aldridge, John
Allen, Peter
Allen, Layton
Allison, Alfred
Allston, William L.
Ames, Allison
Anderson, Patrick H.
Bagby, James S.
Baker, Augustus
Baker, Stephen
Barkley, John H.
Barnhill, John N.
Barton, Thomas B.
Bates, Anthony
Batts, James S.
Beall, Josias B.
Beck, John F
Bell, Marvin
Bellows, Fred J.
Bentley, Henry Hogue
Blackwell, Joseph H.
Blake, Thomas M.
Bouch, Gabriel
Bracey, Leslie G.H.
Bradford, James A.
Brashear, Richard G.
Brister, Nathaniel R.
Brooks, John Sowers
Brown, J. S.
Brown, Oliver
Brown, William S.
Bryson, John M.
Buchley, Daniel
Burbidge, Thomas
Burt, Benjamin F.
Butler, Moses
Bynum, Alfred

Byrne, Matthew
Cain, J. W.
Carabajal, Mariano
Carlisle, George Washington
Carrier, Charles J.
Carroll, Michael F.
Caruthers, Ewing
Cash, George W.
Chadwick, Joseph M.
Chew, John
Chisum, Enoch P. Gains
Churchill, Thomas T.
Clark, Joseph H.
Clark, Seth
Coe, John G.
Coglan, George W.
Cole, William H.
Coleman, Jacob
Colston, William John
Comstock, William
Conrad, Cullen
Conway, Matthew
Cosby, Thomas H.
Cowan, William J.
Cox, Harvey
Cozart, Henderson
Cross, John
Cumming, George W.
Cunningham, John D.
Curtman, George F
Daniell, George Washington
Dasher, Thomas Jefferson
Davidson, Robert T
Davis, George A.
Daws, Walter W.
Day, H. B.
Debicki, Napoleon
Dedrick, George
Dennis, Joseph
DeSpain, Randolph

Devereaux, Michael
Dickerman, William P.
Dickinson, Noah Jr.
Dickson, Abijah Hogan
Dickson, Henry H.
Disney, Richard
Donoho, John
Douglass, Henry L.
Douglas, William G.
Downman, Henry M.
Dubose, William P. B.
Duffield, J. E.
Duncan, James W.
Dusanque, Francis J.
Duval, Burr H.
Dyer, George
Eddy, Andrew H.
Edwards, Samuel M.
Eels, Otis G.
Ellis, James F.
Ellis, Michael
Ely, John
English, Robert
Escott
Eubanks, George
Fadden, John
Fannin, James Walker
Farney, Samuel
Fenner, Robert
Ferguson, Joseph G.
Fine, Charles
Fisher, John H.
Fitzsimmons, Edward
Foley, Arthur G.
Foster, J. A.
Fowler, Bradford
Framer, William Warren
Franklin, Elijah B.
Frazer, Hugh McDonald
Frazer, Charles
Frazier, Micajah G.
Freeman, Thomas S.

Frizzell, Terrell R.
Frost, Hezekiah
Fuller, Edward
Gallagher, Dominic
Gamble, David
Garner, Edward
Garner, M. C.
Gates, Lucius W.
Gatlin, William James
Gibbs, John
Gibbs, Lewis C.
Gilbenrath, Imanuel Frederic
Gilbert, William
Gilkison, Francis
Gilland, George M.
Gimble, John
Gleeson, John
Gould
Grace, John C.
Graves, Ransome O.
Gray, Francis H.
Green, George
Green, William T.
Grimes, James H.
Grinolds, E. J. D.
Gunter, William
Hamilton, James A.
Hand, John J.
Hardwick, Charles S.
Harper, William
Harris, Jesse
Harris, William
Harrison, Erasmus D.
Haskell, Charles Ready
Hastic, Henry
Hatfield, William R.
Hawkins, Norborne B.
Heath, Ebenezer Smith
Helms, Wilson
Hemphill, William
Heyser, John
Hill, Stuart

Hitchard, John
Hodge, Nathan
Hufty, Edward H.
Hughes, Wesley
Hughes, Wiley
Humphries, Jesse C.
Hunt, Francis M.
Hunter, William
Hurst, Stephen Decatur
Jack, James C.
Jackson, John N.
James
James, John
Jennings, Charles B.
Jones, Henry W.
Johnson, David
Johnson, Edward J.
Johnston, William P.
Kelly, James
Kelly, John
Kemp, James P.
King, Montgomery B.
Kinney, Allen O.
Kissam, P. T.
Kornicky, John
Lamond, Adams G.
Lantz, Charles
Lee, Green
Leverett, Oscar F.
Linley, Charles
Logan, John C.
Loverly, Alexander J.
Loving, Joseph S.
Lynch, A. M.
Lynde, A. H.
Mahoney, Dennis
Martin, Henry
Mattern, Peter
Mays, Samuel A. J.
McCoy, James
McDonald, James A.
McGloin, John

McGowan, Dennis
McGowen, John
McKenzie, Kenneth
McKinley, Charles
McLennan, Alexander
McManomy, T. B.
McMurray, William
McSherry, James
Merrifield, William Jefferson
Miller, Isaac H.
Miller, James M.
Mills, Seaborn A.
Milne, Charles C.
Minor, Drury Hugh
Mitchell, Warren Jordan
Mitchell, Washington
Mixon, Claiborne D.
Moat, John
Moody, Edward
Moore, David
Moore, John H.
Moore, John O.
Morgan, John F.
Moses, David
Munson, Charles Rufus
Murdock, David A.
Neven, Patrick
Nobles, Watkins
Noland, James
Numlin, John
Oliver, John M.
O'Neal, Zeno R.
Osborn, Patrick
Owings, Robert Smith
Pace, Robert A.
Paine, George W.
Parker, John K.
Parker, William S.
Parvin, William
Patton, Charles
Penny, George W.
Perkins, Austin

Perkins, D. A. J.
Petrussewicz, A. Adolph
Pettus, Samuel Overton
Petty, Rufus R.
Phillips, Charles
Pierce, Stephen
Pittman, James F.
Pittman, Samuel C.
Powell, Lewis
Powers, John M.
Preusch, William G.
Rainey, Robert R.
Reed, James
Rees, Thomas
Reese, Perry
Reeves, Thomas
Richards, John
Riddell, Samuel
Riddle, Joseph P.
Ripley, Henry D.
Roberts, Thomas H.
Rooney, Cornelius
Rose, Gideon
Rowe, Samuel
Rumley, Thomas
Ryan, Edward
Sanders, Samuel Smith
Sanders, Wade H.
Sargent, Charles
Saunders, James H.
Schultz, Henry Lewis
Scott, R. J.
Sealy, John
Seaton, J. M.
Sevenman, Frederick
Seward, John
Shackelford, Fortunatus S.
Shackelford, William J.
Short, Zachariah H.
Simmons, S.
Simpson, Lawson S.
Slatter, Randolph

Smith, James
Smith, Sidney
Smith, William A.
Spencer, Henry
Sprague, Samuel
Stephens, William
Stevens, Abraham
Stewart, Charles B.
Stovall, Joseph A.
Strunk, Bennett
Taliaferro, Benjamin A.
Tatom, Memory B.
Tatom, Joseph R.
Taylor, Kneeland
Thayer, George J. W.
Thomas, Evans B.
Thorn, John Stephen
Ticknor, Isaac
Tilson, Lewis
Turbeville, Wilkins S.
Tyler, John
Vaughan, James
Vaughan, William E.
Vigal, George Marion
Volckman, Frederick J.
Wadsworth, William A. O.
Waggoner, William
Wallace, A. J.
Wallace, Benjamin C.
Wallace, Samuel P.
Ward, William
Waters, Nicholas B.
Watson, Joseph W.
Weaver, Alman
Webb, James
West, James
Weston, Thomas
Westover, Ira J.
Wheeler, Orlando
Wilder, James S.
Wilkey, Henry
Williams, Abner B.

Williams, James
Williams, Napoleon B.
Wilson, Robert W.
Wilson, Samuel
Wingate, Edward
Winn, James C.
Winningham, William S.
Winship, Stephen
Winter, Andrew
Witt, Hughes

Wood, Henry H.
Wood, John
Wood, William P.
Wren, Allen
Wright, Isaac Newton
Yeamans, Elias Robert
Yeamans, Erastus
Young, Harrison
Young, James O.
Youngblood, Solomon

There is substantial evidence that the name Bell Marvin on this list should be "*Bill Marvin*," and Charles J. Carrier, "*Charles J. Carrer*"; that Thomas T. Churchill should be "*Thomas T. Churchwell*," and John Donoho, "*John Donahoo*"; that John Kornicky is properly "*Isaac Kornicky*," Henry Martin, "*Harvey Martin*," Thomas Reeves, "*Thomas Rives*," and Frederick Sevenman, "*Frederick Seibenman*." The best evidence rule was followed in cases of doubt.

(e) Escaped from the massacre, March 27, 1836:

Allen, Thomas G.
Brenan, William
Brooks, Samuel T.
Butler, Bennett
Cooper, Dillard
Devenny, Neill John
Duval, John Crittenden
Ehrenberg, Herman
Haddin, William
Hamilton, Isaac D.
Hazen, Nathaniel
Hicks, Joseph W.
Holland, Benjamin H.

Holliday, John C.
Hunter, William
Jones, David J.
Kemp, Thomas
Mason, William
Martindale, Daniel
Murphy, Daniel
Rees, John
Shain, Charles B.
Sharpe, Augustus V.
Simpson, Wilson
Van Bibber, Sidney
Williams, John

Allen, Brown, Ehrenberg, Hamilton, Mason, and Rees were recaptured after having escaped, before reaching the Texas settlements, and were detained by the enemy from a few weeks to many months before they again escaped or were released. Devenny, Hamilton, Hunter, and Martindale escaped despite having received serious wounds.

(f) Men spared at Goliad, March 27, 1836.

Barnard, Dr. Joseph H.
Boyle, Andrew Michael
Field, Dr. Joseph E.
Fagan, Nicholas
Garcia, Francisco
Griffin, Peter
Hughes, Benjamin H.
Hughes, James
Morgan, Abel

Pittuck, George
Rosenbury, William
Scurlock, William
Shackelford, Dr. Jack
Smith, Charles
Spohn, Joseph H.
Vose, John George Andrew
White, Alvin E.
Wuthrich, Ulrich

Morgan's enlistment and the official references to his being spared at Goliad are in the name of "Thomas Smith." James Hughes, who had been Colonel Fannin's Comissary, was spared under the name "Bills." He died at Goliad after a short illness, before the other Texan prisoners escaped. Vose was later a "Bexar" prisoner. Rosenbury was killed as a member of the Santa Fe Expedition, and White was again captured by the enemy at Mier. Nicholas Fagan and Francis Dieterich, after having been spared at Refugio on March 16 were at Goliad, as prisoners, on March 27, and were again spared.

(g) Men of Colonel Fannin's command not killed or captured because absent, March 14-27, 1836, due to illness or duty:

Barton, John
Bullock, Munroe
Burke, David N.
Dickinson, Robert
Early, Francis
Fagan, John
Good, Isham J.
Hopkins, Joseph
Howe, Joseph
Kenyon, Amos D.
Lamar, Basil

Lowary, John
Magee, Dr. William H.
McNelly, Bennett
Patton, Alexander E.
Smith, John
Tennant, Simpson
Thornton, Francis W.
Van Bibber, John
Washington, Lewis M. H.
Williams, Joseph T.

(h) Possibly killed with Colonel Fannin's command:

Chambers, John L.
Eadock, Henry H.
Hamlet, Richard Green

Ward, Henry L.
Ward, John

Most of these men came to Texas with Captain Peyton S. Wyatt's company, but were not returned as members of that company, nor of any other company, on Colonel Fannin's muster rolls for February 29-March 1, 1836. Eadock, or Eddick, and John Ward signed the memorial of the volunteers at Refugio to the Washington convention about February 5, after Captain Wyatt's departure for the United States. The heirs of Chambers, and of both Wards (not related), were granted bounty and donation lands for their having been "Killed with Fannin," on proof that these soldiers came to Texas with Captain Wyatt's Company; never returned and were never heard from by friends or relatives after the killing of Fannin's men. Hamlet's heirs made similar proof. Nothing has been found in the official records or elsewhere, to explain their fate.

In Goliad, only a few hundred yards from the fortress at La Bahía, which Fannin named Fort Defiance, there is a granite memorial erected in memory of those executed on that Palm Sunday morning. Although there are 342 names inscribed, it is possible there were actually more, and the exact number of dead may never be known.

18

THE SUMMING UP

The Texas War of Independence against Mexico ended on April 21, 1836, when, in a battle on the plains of San Jacinto, at Buffalo Bayou, near present-day Houston, General Santa Anna finally came to grips with his antagonist and fellow general, Sam Houston. The battle was no contest, lasting only eighteen minutes, during which the Texas army of approximately 780 effectives completely routed Santa Anna's forces totaling more than four times that number.

Now that the war is over, the guns are stilled, the smoke has cleared from the battlefields and all the participants on both sides have been long gone, let us examine two of the main characters of this book: President-Dictator General Antonio López de Santa Anna y Perez de Lebron of Mexico, and one of his major opponents, Col. James Walker Fannin, Jr. Both, as military commanders, made serious mistakes. For Santa Anna his mistakes cost Mexico the area of Texas, which then was far, far larger than it is today. It also cost him the unnecessary loss of hundreds of his men's lives. For poor Fannin, the mistakes cost him his life and the lives of approximately 340 of his troops.

Perhaps the most serious blunder of all made by Santa Anna was his ordering the execution of Fannin and all of his troops at Goliad. Prior to this senseless slaughter, the cause of the Texans was viewed with little sympathy by many of the people in the

United States. But when news of the execution of men of Goliad reached the United States, there was a wave of revulsion against Santa Anna and Mexico, and sympathy for the unfortunates whose rifles had been taken. Public opinion in the United States and in other nations in the world definitely turned in favor of the Texans, as they regarded the massacre with disgust and contempt.

Many people in Texas, later on, believed that the postscript on the surrender document bearing Urrea's signature was added long after he and Santa Anna had returned to Mexico. Some weight must be given their belief because Colonel Holsinger, in a letter he wrote John A. Wharton the following June, says that Urrea told Fannin that he could rely on Mexican clemency, and gave his personal assurance that the men's lives would be spared. However, Urrea rode on to Victoria and made no intercession with Santa Anna for the clemency he promised.

Santa Anna, in his ego, called himself the "Napoleon of the West" and the "Hero of Tampico," but it is highly unlikely the former emperor of France would have looked with satisfaction upon the appellation the Mexican president bestowed upon himself, as in his military career Santa Anna displayed few, if any, of the qualities of genius the real Napoleon displayed.

All good commanders know that they should take care of their men, particularly the enlisted troops. Santa Anna cared little or nothing about his men, and less about the enlisted personnel. When he left his headquarters in Mexico to start his campaign he failed to take along a medical corps or any doctors, surgeons, nurses, or medical supplies.

One of the first lessons good commanders learn is to keep in close touch with their immediate subordinates. Here again the Mexican dictator fouled up. He placed his second-in-command, Major General Filisola, at the rear of a 300-mile procession, as a caboose is at the rear of a train. And this in an era of no telephones, telegraphs, or radios. This created a severe waste of time and confusion with couriers riding back and forth with messages from master to deputy and deputy to master.

With so many residents of Texas being Mexicans whose sympathies were not with the Anglos but with the Mexican government, Santa Anna and his army had excellent intelligence as to where the various units of the Texas army were, their strength, and what they were up to.

There was no earthly military or political necessity for pressing on to San Antonio to storm the Alamo after once reaching the Rio Grande. In vain did Santa Anna's senior commanders advise him to avoid that fort and concentrate on more worthy military objectives. And those commanders knew what they were talking about, inasmuch as some of them had served under the great master, Napoleon, himself during the latter's campaigns. As Enrique de la Pena, an engineer on his staff, exclaimed: "Santa Anna needed a century of instruction to match the wisdom of his senior officers."

Politically, the Alamo was nothing. Militarily, until just a few days before the fortress fell, William Barret Travis had only around 150 men in the place until his troops were swelled by the thirty-two men from Gonzales. Santa Anna would have been far better off to send a few hundred men to the Alamo and bottle up Travis and starve him out, thereby saving more than 600 of his own army.

Santa Anna had much better choices to put his army to use. At the time he arrived at San Antonio his chief opponent, Houston, was not with the Texas army; he was with the Indians negotiating a peace treaty. The Mexican general should have sent his army to Gonzales or Victoria in an effort to wipe out what few troops the Texans had at those places. And Fannin, holed up in his Fort Defiance, presented a tempting target indeed. With far less numbers than *el presidente* had, he was also short on food, ammunition, and supplies. A detachment of sufficient size could have marched to La Bahía and with little difficulty bottled up Fannin and his defenders and starved them into submission.

At Buffalo Bayou, where Santa Anna met his version of the real Napoleon's Waterloo, the dictator could hardly have chosen a worse spot to make his stand against the Texans. His rear was protected by an extensive grove of trees, but he was bounded on the south and east by a vast marsh, which gave him no room to maneuver or retreat. Several of his officers thought that the spot chosen to fight was ridiculous, and one later commented any youngster could have done better. Once again Santa Anna disregarded this advice.

To cap it off, Santa Anna and his troops took their usual three o'clock *siesta* and that is exactly when Sam Houston chose to strike. De la Pena evidently thought that was not the fair way to fight a war, as in his diary he later wrote that he thought "it was reprehensible of Houston to attack when the Mexicans were enjoying their *siesta*."

When the attack broke, Santa Anna was in his marquee and, if the reports are correct, was being entertained by a mulatto he had commandeered a few days previously. Whether or not he was being entertained is immaterial, but it is true that when the attack and the fighting began in earnest, the "Napoleon of the West" grabbed the first horse he came to and instead of trying to rally his troops, fled the scene in his drawers as fast as he could, leaving his army to shift for itself. His opponent, Houston, was point man and led his troops into action on his white horse, Saracen, who was shot from under him. Houston quickly mounted another horse, and it too was shot from under him. In the process the general was severely wounded in the right ankle. For the third time he mounted a horse and was still in the action when the battle was over.

A slight difference in commanders.

James Walker Fannin, Jr., of Georgia, is an authentic Texas hero but of the second echelon when compared to others such as Houston, Bowie, Travis, Milam, and others. One reason for this is that he committed the unpardonable sin among military commanders. He got beaten. True, Travis and Bowie were beaten and lost their lives, but they went down fighting, and Milam lost his life while actively engaged in combat.

One of the first officers to be commissioned in the regular army of the Provisional Government, he was given the high rank of full colonel and swore an oath of obedience to the Provisional Government and to his military superiors. From the first he promptly disregarded many orders given him by Sam Houston, his superior as commanding general of the army. When the split occurred between Governor Henry Smith and Lieutenant Governor James W. Robinson and other members of the government, Fannin promptly sided with the dissidents.

Fannin was a brave and compassionate man, and he met his

execution with dignity. As a humane person he deserves to be given full credit for sending first King and then Ward to Refugio to bring the stranded colonists back to Goliad. But he made a terrible mistake in tactics by dividing his force almost in half, as he should have remembered that his troops came first. He should have more promptly followed Houston's orders to retreat to Victoria, and let King, Ward, and the colonists catch up with him if they could.

As commander at Fort Defiance, Fannin exhibited indecision, procrastination, and a "fortress mentality," and he would not budge from his sacred garrison until it was too late. The history of warfare shows that armies on the defensive seldom win, and armies holed up in forts never do as their fort can eventually be taken by greater numbers, surrounded and starved out, or allowed to just die on the vine. It was not until March 10 that Fannin received any substantial munitions, supplies, and food, and once he had his provisions he should have moved out to Victoria, or taken his action-eager army and met Urrea in the field. But Fannin, with more than 400 men with him, did nothing but sit and wait.

It is to his credit that, although he knew it was a forlorn hope, he finally moved to reach San Antonio to assist Travis, but the amateurish way his army started off compelled them to return home.

Fannin's indecisiveness, hesitation, and procrastination was observed by his troops and caused him to lose popularity with them and their respect, and consequently a loss of effectiveness as a commander. And then when he finally decided to obey Houston and retreat to Victoria, he delayed unnecessarily for several days. The march out of the fort, when it finally began, revealed nothing but amateurishness and inefficiency. Food was forgotten, wagons overloaded so that many broke down, and worst of all, despite the entreaties of his senior subordinates, nothing would do but they had to stop on the plains and relax when protective woods and much needed water were only a few hundred yards away. This final blunder proved fatal and cost him not only his life but the lives of his army as well.

And so poor Fannin, who had started out on his war with such high hopes, met his end. The fact that he fought and died bravely for his country entitles him to a place in the Pantheon of Honor in Texas, but his many weaknesses as a leader have clouded his reputation. On the contrary, the reputations of William Barret Travis, Jim Bowie, Davy Crockett, James Butler Bonham, Ben Milam, and others of his comrades-in-arms who lost their lives remain untarnished.

Epilogue

When the ragged Texas army defeated the troops of Santa Anna in the Battle of San Jacinto on April 21, 1836, Gen. Sam Houston assumed the point and was in advance of his troops when the attack began. Having twice had his mounts shot out from under him and being seriously wounded above the right ankle, the general was on his third horse and still in the fray when the battle was over.

After the war, Houston served as first president of the Republic of Texas. Constitutionally unable to succeed himself, he retired from politics and after the term of Mirabeau B. Lamar, his successor, was again elected as president. When, in 1845, Texas entered the Union, he and Thomas J. Rusk were the first two senators elected, and served almost fourteen years before returning home. Defeated for governor on his first attempt, he was elected to that office on his second try. After Texas seceded from the Union, Houston was ousted as governor by the Texas Legislature when he refused to take an oath of allegiance to the Confederacy. He died of pneumonia on July 26, 1863, at his residence in Huntsville.

Stephen F. Austin, the "Father of Texas," was appointed by Houston as secretary of state of the new republic. Hard-working and industrious, he was an excellent choice for that position. A lifelong bachelor, Austin died in office of pneumonia on December 27, 1837.

Thomas Jefferson Rusk was a friend of Houston's prior to the war, when they were lawyers in Nacogdoches. Under the Provisional Government, Rusk served as secretary of war and with the rank of colonel was engaged in the Battle of San Jacinto. After the end of hostilities, when Houston went to New Orleans on leave to have his ankle injury treated, Rusk succeeded him as commander-in-chief of the army. Appointed as the first secretary of war under Houston, he also briefly served as secretary of state when Austin died, and later became chief justice of the Supreme Court of Texas while it was a republic. He served as a senator from Texas in the United States Senate along with Houston until, suffering from a severe depression after his wife Polly died, he committed suicide on July 29, 1857.

James W. Robinson, who had served so disastrously as lieutenant-governor in the Provisional Government, had found no place for him in the ad interim government nor the new republic. In September 1842, Robinson was in San Antonio when the city was attacked by a force of 1,200 Mexicans under the command of Gen. Adrian Woll, a French soldier of fortune who, like so many European officers, served in Santa Anna's army. Robinson was captured along with about fifty other men and quickly found himself languishing in a Mexican prison. Finally, by a clever ruse and with the help of Sam Houston, he managed to persuade Santa Anna to release him. Once more he disappeared into oblivion.

Santa Anna had many political lives. Recalled from exile in 1846, once more he became president of Mexico and then commander-in-chief of the army in the Mexican-American War. After being defeated in the stubbornly contested Battle of Buena Vista in February 1847, he retired to Jamaica. Recalled by a revolution in 1853, he once more became president of Mexico. His harsh rule produced a number of revolts, and in 1855 he was driven from the country, finally finding a refuge in St. Thomas. He died in 1876.

Francita Alavez, better known as the Angel of Goliad, was the wife of Capt. Telesforo Alavez, a cavalry officer under General Urrea. Captain Alavez had a legitimate wife and two small children whom he had abandoned in 1834. After the war with Texas was over, the Angel of Goliad returned to Mexico City with Captain Alavez, who abandoned her. Without any funds she returned to Matamoros, where she found many warm friends. According to Bill and Marjorie K. Walraven in their book *The Magnificent Barbarians*, she returned to Texas later with her children and is buried on the famous King Ranch, where her son worked for Capt. Richard King.

Hugh McDonald Frazer is one of those listed on the monument at Goliad as being among those executed on Santa Anna's orders. That is not correct. Frazer and his company rendered yeoman service to Fannin in scouting and reconnaissance. After the Battle of Coleto Plains, Frazer, whose company as such was not in the battle, together with several of his men made their way to Gonzales and joined Houston's army. Under the command of Houston, they were in the Battle of San Jacinto.

Dr. John (Jack) Shackelford was born in Virginia on March 20, 1790; consequently the surrender of Fannin and his men occurred on his forty-sixth birthday. Shackelford served in the War of 1812 and then moved to Courtland, Alabama, where he raised a company of "Red Rovers" and led them to Texas. After the war he returned to Alabama, where he died in 1857. Shackelford County, Texas, is named for him.

Dr. Joseph Henry Barnard stayed in the Texas army and from June 10 until October 28, 1836, served as post surgeon at Galveston. While engaged in this duty Dr. Barnard assisted in preparing the roll of Fannin's men published by the *Telegraph and Texas Register*, November 9, 1836.

Dr. Barnard was county clerk of Fort Bend County in 1838-39 and in 1843-44 represented that county in the House of the Eighth Congress. In 1838 he married Mrs. Nancy N. Handy, a widow, by whom he had three children. In 1858 he served as a member of the Texas Legislature and in 1860 returned to his native Canada for a visit. He died there in the latter part of December 1860, or the very early part of January 1861, and was buried there.

Francis W. Johnson, one of the leaders of the ill-fated Matamoros Expedition, retired from the Texas army after his defeat from Urrea. He died in Mexico in 1884.

Capt. Philip Dimitt died in a Mexican dungeon in 1841. Maj. Gen. Vicente Filisola, the Italian-born second-in-command to Santa Anna, became commander-in-chief of the Mexican army after the capture and surrender of Santa Anna. He returned to Mexico and subsequently was court-martialed for having obeyed Santa Anna's orders to evacuate Texas. In defense of his actions he wrote his *"Representation to the Supreme Government with Notes on His Operations as General-in-Chief of the Army of Texas,"* and his *"Memoirs For The History Of The War In Texas."* Filisola was exonerated at his court-martial, and died in Mexico City on July 23, 1850, at the age of sixty-one. His cause of death was due to cholera, which he developed during an epidemic.

After leaving Fannin, Capt. William G. Cooke served on Houston's staff at the Battle of San Jacinto. In 1844 he was married to Angela Navarro, daughter of the distinguished José Antonio Navarro, for whom Navarro County is named. Cooke later became a general on the Confederate side during the Civil War, and Cooke County is named for him.

Col. Albert Clinton Horton was a native of Georgia but moved to Alabama, where he became a member of the legislature. Leaving Alabama, he moved to Texas as a colonist and prospered. After the war he became wealthy and was a co-founder and incorporator of Baylor University, and then became the first lieutenant-governor of Texas when the republic became a state.

Herman Ehrenberg was born in Marienwerder, Prussia, about 1818 and came to the United States while still a boy. On June 2, 1836, he received an honorable discharge from the army by Mirabeau B. Lamar, who was secretary of war in the ad-interim government. He later traveled the Pacific Ocean for a few years and returned to California to fight against the Mexicans, and to witness the gold rush of 1849. In 1853 he was engaged in mining enterprises in Arizona, and made the first map of the Gadsden Purchase; in 1856 he became engineer and surveyor for the Sonora Exploring and Mining Company, and around 1862 settled at La Paz on the Colorado River, where he lived the remainder of his life. He later became an Indian agent for the Mohaves on the Colorado River Reservation and was killed, probably by Indians, in October 1866, at Dos Palmas, California, on the road between his home and San Bernardino.

His memoirs concerning his activities in the Texas war were first published in Leipsig in 1843 as *Texas Und Seine Revolution*.

John Crittendon Duval was born in Kentucky in 1816 and came to Texas with his brother Burr. After the war in Texas he joined his parents, who were then living in Florida as his father was the territorial governor. He then completed his education at the University of Virginia and returned to Texas.

As early as 1845 Duval was a member of Capt. Jack Hays' company of Texas Rangers, along with Big-Foot Wallace. He later took up surveying for a livelihood and when the Civil War broke out, enlisted in the Confederate army, and served two years in Alabama, Georgia, and Tennessee.

After the Civil War, Duval spent some years in New Mexico as a surveyor, living among the Pueblo Indians along the Rio Grande. In 1876 he began work as a surveyor for the International and Great Northern Railroad Company. In his later years he lived in Austin, and was buried there after dying in 1897.

The Presidio La Bahía was restored in 1966 and sits in an open countryside, a couple of miles from the city of Goliad. It is now owned and kept up by the Catholic Church, and the fortress has been preserved about exactly as it was when Colonel Fannin and his troops were there. About 300 yards from the presidio is a memorial marker, and on the walls it lists all the names of those massacred. The remains of Fannin and his men were buried at the site of the marker by Thomas J. Rusk and his men.

Mrs. James Fannin, the former Minerva Fort, and her two daughters, Pinckney and Minerva, were received in the home of William H. Jack, near Velasco, after the death of the colonel. Mrs. Fannin died in 1837 and Pinckney, the youngest daughter, followed her in death in 1847 at the age of fifteen. Minerva was committed to the Texas State Asylum in Austin in 1862 as a mental patient. Upon her death on July 27, 1893, she was buried in the State Cemetery.

Both Fannin County and the town of Fannin, in Goliad County, are named for the colonel.

NOTES

CHAPTER 1

1. H. Yoakum, *History of Texas,* I, 334.

2. Eugene C. Barker, *Mexico and Texas 1821-1825,* 56.

3. John Austin was no relation to Stephen F. Austin.

4. Bradburn returned to Texas in 1836 as part of Santa Anna's army and was in the Battle of San Jacinto. Being in one of the rear divisions, he was not killed or taken prisoner.

5. Amelia W. Williams and Eugene C. Barker, eds., *The Writings of Sam Houston,* I, 302-303.

6. Hobart Huson, *Captain Phillip Dimitt's Commandancy of Goliad,* 22.

7. Fannin to David Mills, Caney Creek, Sept. 18, 1835. *Austin Papers,* III, 126, 127.

8. Huson, xxii.

9. John L. Linn, *Reminiscences of Fifty Years in Texas,* 119, 120.

CHAPTER 2

1. There are many versions as to who actually invented the famous Bowie knife. Some authorities contend that Jim Bowie, in a fight, cut his hand by striking such a blow with a knife that his fingers slipped down upon the blade and thereupon he devised a knife with a hilt. Others contend that it was his brother Rezin who had the fight and whose hand was cut and who then invented the knife. Another version is that the first Bowie knife as we know it today—one with a crossguard—was actually the invention of a famous knife-maker named James Black of Hempstead, Arkansas. This version has quite a bit of credibility to it. In all likelihood the knife may have been invented years

153

before the Bowies came along. Regardless of who actually invented this weapon, it was the ferocity with which Jim Bowie wielded it in combat that gave it its name. This knife had a length of twelve and one-half inches with a blade of eight inches and a width of one and one-half inches. Due to the wide publicity given the exploits of Bowie and his knife, demand for it became so great that in Sheffield, England, a factory was built to manufacture them for the Texas market.

2. Jim Bowie was on an extended trip east to Natchez, Mississippi, when, between September 5 and 8, 1833, his family died from cholera at Monclova, in the Coahuila section, where the Veramendis had a summer home. Bowie has not aware of the catastrophe when he executed his will at Natchez on October 21, 1833. In it he designated as his sole heirs his brother Rezin P. Bowie and their sister Martha Bowie Sterrett and her husband, Alexander B. Sterrett. His wife, he explained, had already been provided for. He stipulated that $4,000 be restored to a friend who had advanced him that sum, and $4,000 more be given another friend who had secured a loan to him for that amount. The deaths made, in ascending order, Ursula Bowie's grandmother, a Navarro, inheritor of the whole Veramendi estate. She died in 1837, leaving other Navarros to inherit and to make claims against the Bowie estate.

3. *Texas State Historical Association Quarterly*, 9, No. 4, 227-230.

4. *Ibid.*, 232.

5. Charles Edwards Lester, *The Life of Sam Houston: The Only Authentic Memoir of Him Ever Published*, 69.

6. Eugene C. Barker, *The Life of Stephen F. Austin*, 417.

7. Clarence Wharton, *Remember Goliad*, 26.

CHAPTER 3

1. Marquis James, *The Raven*, 181.

2. Andrew Jackson Houston, *Texas Independence*, 91.

3. Fannin to Governor Smith, November [31] sic, 1835, Texas State Archives, D, file 6, No. 555.

4. Huson, *Captain Phillip Dimitt's Commandancy of Goliad*, 165-167.

5. *Ibid.*, 172, 173.

6. Jakie L. Pruett and Everett B. Cole, Sr., *Goliad Massacre*, 22.

7. Harbert Davenport, *Southwestern Historical Quarterly*, 43:9.

8. Williams and Barker, *Writings*, I, 322-323.

9. *Ibid.*

10. Davenport, *Southwestern Historical Quarterly*, 43:8.

11. Clifford Hopewell, *Sam Houston: Man of Destiny*, 173.

12. Houston, 97.

CHAPTER 4

1. Williams and Barker, *Writings*, I, 334.

2. Yoakum, II, 58, and Order to Bowie, January 17, 1836.

3. Williams and Barker, *Writings*, I, 339.

4. Dr. Joseph E. Field, *Three Years in Texas*, 26.

CHAPTER 5

1. James M. Day, *Battles of Texas*, 43.
2. José Enrique de la Pena, *With Santa Anna in Texas*, translated and edited by Carmen Perry, 68.
3. Williams and Barker, *Writings*, I, 342.
4. Peach Tree Village in Tyler County, Texas, was named because of an enormous peach tree orchard there. It was the principal village of the Alabama-Coushatta tribe, who were in the same Indian confederation as the Cherokees. The Alabama-Coushatta Reservation is on U.S. Highway 190, about fifty miles from Huntsville, Texas, and is between Livingston and Woodville. On the reservation today is a marker signifying where Sam Houston and the Indians from the various tribes met and signed their treaty.
5. T. R. Fehrenbach, *Lone Star*, 204.
6. Joe B. Frantz, et al., *Heroes of Texas,* 129. Somerfield Edition.
7. Virgil E. Baugh, *Rendezvous at the Alamo*, 97.
8. José Enrique de la Pena, 18.

CHAPTER 6

1. Harbert Davenport, "The Men of Goliad," *Southwestern Historical Quarterly*, Vol. 43, No. 1, July 1939.
2. *Ibid.*, 16.
3. *Ibid.*, 17.
4. *Ibid.*

CHAPTER 7

1. Hobart Huson, ed., *Dr. Joseph Henry Barnard's Journal*, Golden Centennial Edition, 1949, 5.
2. Texana was formerly named Santa Anna, but after hostilities commenced, the name of the town was changed.
3. Huson, ed., *Dr. Joseph Henry Barnard's Journal*, 9, 10.
4. *Ibid.*, 12.
5. Davenport, "The Men of Goliad," *Southwestern Historical Quarterly*, 43: 18.
6. Houston, *Texas Independence*, 111.
7. Roy Grimes, *Goliad 130 Years After*, 22.
8. Herman Ehrenberg, *With Milam and Fannin: The Adventures of a German Boy in Texas' Revolution*, 143d.
9. Pruett and Cole, *Goliad Massacre*, 34.
10. Yoakum, 2:81.

CHAPTER 8

1. Houston, *Texas Independence*, 114.
2. Wharton, *Remember Goliad,* 26.
3. Houston, 114.
4. *Ibid.*
5. Henry Stuart Foote, *Texas and the Texans*, 2:214.
6. Eugene C. Barker, *History of Texas*, 283, 284.

7. Ruth Cumby Smith, "James W. Fannin, Jr., in the Texas Revolution," *Southwestern Historical Quarterly*, 23: 200-202.

8. Linn, *Reminiscences of Fifty Years in Texas*, 127.

9. Huson, ed., *Dr. Joseph Henry Barnard's Journal*, 14.

10. Ehrenberg, 154.

CHAPTER 9

1. Houston, 130.

2. *Ibid.*, 131.

3. José Enrique de la Pena, 36, 39.

4. Baugh, 204, 205.

5. Hopewell, 185.

6. Charles Edwards Lester, *The Life of Sam Houston: The Only Authentic Memoir of Him Ever Published*, 90, 91.

7. Houston, 133.

8. Among the few survivors from the Alamo were Mrs. Susannah Dickinson, wife of Capt. Almeron Dickinson, an artilleryman from Tennessee, and her fifteen-month-old daughter Angelina; and Joe, Travis' black body servant. There was a Mexican named Gregorio Esparza who served under Travis and Bowie and perished at the Alamo. He had taken his wife and four children into the Alamo and they survived. His son, Enrique, as a young lad had fallen into the San Antonio River and been saved from drowning by James Bowie. Young Enrique lived to be a very old man, and the May 12, 1907, edition of *The San Antonio Daily Express* carried his eyewitness account of the battle.

Fifteen-year-old Gertrudis Navarro and her older married sister, Juana Navarro Alsbury, were cousins of Bowie's wife Ursula. Mrs. Alsbury had her eighteen-month-old son, Alijo, with her and all of them survived. Over the years it seems as if a few soldiers survived the battle as some, thought dead, had been wounded and somehow survived.

During recent years some evidence has been produced to show that contrary to the generally accepted figure of 188 victims at the Alamo, the total may actually have been much higher—perhaps as many as 245 to 250. These figures have not so far been confirmed.

According to the diary of de la Pena, the Mexican women told Santa Anna that for some days the men under Travis' command had been urging him to surrender, as in spite of all his appeals for aid none had been forthcoming with the exception of the men from Gonzales, and that supplies were getting short. On the fifth, Travis had promised them that if no help arrived on that day they would surrender the next day, or try to escape under darkness. The Texans were in communication with some of their sympathizers in San Antonio, and that Santa Anna had gotten wind of that decision by Travis. It was for this reason that he precipitated the assault when he did.

CHAPTER 10

1. Richard G. Santos, *Santa Anna's Campaign Against Texas*, 35. The infantry's equipment was predominately British; English flintlock rifles firing a 1 1/2 oz. ball, ramrods, flints, locks, bayonets, steel saber and scabbards, and even British brass drums. The alternate rifle was a British Baker flint ignition

gun weighing 9.5 pounds without bayonet, 3'9 1/2 inches in length, with a 30-inch barrel of .615 caliber firing a 350 grain bullet at 1,200 feet per second, with sighting to 200 yards.

2. Ramon Martinez Caro, secretary to Santa Anna, in Castaneda, trans., *The Mexican Side of the Texas Revolution*, 104.

3. Account furnished by Mrs. Dickinson, *Telegraph and Texas Register*, March 24, 1836.

4. Hopewell, 190.

5. According to an official list of names provided by the Daughters of the Republic of Texas at the Alamo, San Antonio.

6. *The Alamo-Long Barrack Museum*, 42. Compiled by the Daughters of the Republic of Texas, 1986.

7. *Ibid.*, 36.

8. *Ibid.*, 42.

9. Fehrenbach, 214.

10. Smith, 23:199.

11. *Ibid.*, 197.

12. Foote, 2:216-218.

13. Letter, Robinson to Fannin. Texas State Archives.

14. Ehrenherg, 151, 152.

15. Letter, Fannin to Mexia. From collection of the Center for American History, University of Texas at Austin.

16. Huson, ed., *Dr. Joseph Henry Barnard's Journal*, 14.

17. Davenport, "The Men of Goliad," *Southwestern Historical Quarterly*, 43: 13.

18. Houston, 114.

CHAPTER 11

1. M. K. Wisehart, *Sam Houston: American Giant*, 173.

2. Desauque stayed with Fannin and was one of the men who was later executed.

3. Pruett and Cole, 144.

4. *Ibid.*, 145.

5. Houston, 168.

6. Sabina Brown, memoirs dictated to an amanuensis.

7. *Ibid.*

8. Pruett and Cole, 55. *The Colorado Gazette and Advertiser*, January 25, 1840.

CHAPTER 12

1. José Enrique de la Pena, 70. Maj. Gen. Vicente Filisola, Santa Anna's Italian-born second-in-command, in his *Memorias para la Guerra de Tejas*, II, 410-414, used Col. Francisco Garay's diary of the events of March 14 as his source. He states General Urrea marched against the mission with 200 infantry, 200 cavalry, and the cannon.

2. Yoakum, 2:87.

3. Urrea, Diary, in Castaneda, trans., *The Mexican Side of the Texas Revolution*, 222.

4. Ehrenberg, 169.
5. Lester Hamilton, *Goliad Survivor Isaac D. Hamilton*, 32.

CHAPTER 13
1. Huson, ed., *Dr. J. H. Barnard's Journal*, 16, 17.
2. Yoakum, 2:87.
3. Urrea, Diary, in Castaneda, trans., *The Mexican Side of the Texas Revolution*, 222.
4. Ehrenberg, 169.
5. Lester Hamilton, *Goliad Survivor Isaac D. Hamilton*, 32.
6. Ehrenberg, 170.
7. Houston, 175, 176.

CHAPTER 14
1. Yoakum, 2:94.
2. Urrea, Diary, in Castaneda, trans., *The Mexican Side of the Texas Revolution*, 224.
3. Houston, 176.
4. Yoakum, 2:93.
5. Urrea, 227.
6. Ehrenberg, 175.
7. William Kennedy, *Texas*, 572.
8. Huson, ed., *Dr. Joseph Henry Barnard's Journal*, 26.
9. Urrea, 228.
10. Huson, 21.
11. Yoakum, 2:522-523.
12. *Ibid.*

CHAPTER 15
1. Huson, ed., *Dr. Joseph Henry Barnard's Journal*, 28, 29.
2. Abel Morgan, *An Account of the Battle of Goliad and Fannin's Massacre*, Texas State Archives.
3. Wisehart, 201.
4. Yoakum, 2:517.
5. From the diary of Colonel Portilla, in Casteneda, *The Mexican Side of the Texas Revolution*, 244.
6. Castaneda, *The Mexican Side of the Texas Revolution*, 107.

CHAPTER 16
1. Huson, ed., *Dr. Joseph Henry Barnard's Journal*, 31, 32.
2. Ehrenberg, 200-204.
3. *Ibid.*, 207-224.
4. John C. Duval, *Early Times in Texas*, 268-271.
5. Pruett and Cole, 114.
6. Excerpt from a newspaper article in the Texas State Archives.
7. Kathryn Stoner O'Connor, *Presidio La Bahía*, 143-145. The watch was later obtained by Capt. William H. Jack and then by Dr. Tomlinson Fort, a relative of Fannin's wife, Minerva Fort Fannin. It became part of the Summerfield

G. Roberts Collection, and is now in the Hall of State Building on the grounds of the State Fair of Texas at Dallas.

8. *Ibid.*, 269. Hughes grew up and died in Dallas sixty years later, leaving an account of his experiences.

9. Huson, ed., *Dr. Joseph Henry Barnard's Journal*, 36.

BIBLIOGRAPHY

BOOKS

Barker, Eugene C. *Mexico and Texas 1821-1835*. Dallas: P. L. Turner Company, 1928.

————. *The Life of Stephen F. Austin*. University of Texas Press, 1980.

————, ed. *Texas History*. Dallas: The Southwest Press, 1929.

Baugh, Virgil E. *Rendezvous at the Alamo*. New York: Pageant Press, Inc., 1960.

Castaneda, Carlos E., trans. *The Mexican Side of the Texas Revolution*, 1836. By the Chief Mexican Participants. Dallas: P. L. Turner Company, 1928.

Crawford, Ann Fears, ed. *The Eagle, The Autobiography of Santa Anna*. Austin: Pemberton Press, 1967.

Day, James M. *Battles of Texas*. Waco: Texian Press, 1967.

————, et al. *Heroes of Texas*. Waco: Texian Press, 1964.

de la Pena, Jose Enrique. *With Santa Anna in Texas*. College Station: Texas A&M University Press, 1975.

Duval, John C. *Early Times in Texas*. Dallas: Tandy Publishing Company, Inc., 1936.

Ehrenberg, Herman. *With Milam and Fannin — Adventures of a German Boy in Texas' Revolution*. Austin: The Pemberton Press, 1968.

Fehrenbach, T. R. *Lone Star, A History of Texas and the Texans*. New York: American Legacy Press, 1983.

Field, Dr. Joseph E. *Three Years in Texas*. Greenfield, MA: Justin Jones, 1836. Reprinted by The Steck Company, Austin, 1935.

Filisola, Don Vicente. *Memoirs For the History of the War in Texas*. Vol. 2, Translated by Wallace Woolsey, 1848. Austin: Eakin Press, 1985.

Frantz, Joe. B. *Texas, A Bicentennial History*. New York: W. W. Norton & Company, Inc., 1976.

——, et al. *Heroes of Texas*. Waco: Texian Press, 1964.

Grimes, Roy. *Goliad 130 Years After*. Victoria, Texas: The Victoria Advocate Publishing Company, 1966.

Hamilton, Lester. *Goliad Survivor Isaac D. Hamilton*. San Antonio: The Naylor Company, 1971.

Hopewell, Clifford. *Sam Houston: Man of Destiny*. Austin: Eakin Press, 1987.

Houston, Andrew Jackson, *Texas Independence*. Houston: Anson Jones Press, 1938.

Huson, Hobart. *Captain Phillip Dimitt's Commandancy of Goliad, 1835-1836*. Austin: Von Boeckmann-Jones Co., 1974.

——, ed., *Dr. Joseph Henry Barnard's Journal*. Refugio: Golden Centennial Edition, 1949.

James, Marquis. *The Raven*. Indianapolis: Bobbs-Merrill Company, 1929.

Kennedy, William. *Texas: The Rise, Progress and Prospects of the Republic of Texas*. Fort Worth: The Molyneau Craftsman, Inc., 1925.

Lester, Charles Edward. *The Life of Sam Houston: The Only Authentic Memoir of Him Ever Published*. New York: J. C Derby, 1855.

Linn, John J. *Reminiscences of Fifty Years in Texas*. Austin: State House Press, 1968.

McDonald, Archie P. *Travis*. Austin: Jenkins Publishing Company, Pemberton Press, 1976.

Nance, Joseph Milton. *Attack and Counter-Attack*. Austin: The University of Texas Press, 1964.

——, et al. *Heroes of Texas*. Waco: Texian Press, 1964.

O'Connor, Kathryn Stoner. *Presidio La Bahia*. Austin: Von Boeckmann-Jones Co., 1966.

Pruett, Jakie L., and Everett B. Cole, Jr. *Goliad Massacre: A Tragedy of the Texas Revolution*. Austin: Eakin Press, 1985.

Santos, Richard G. *Santa Anna's Campaign Against Texas, 1835-1836. Featuring the Field Commands Issued to Major General Vicente Filisola*. Waco: Texian Press, 1968.

Tolbert, Frank X. *The Day of San Jacinto*. Austin and New York: Pemberton Press, 1969.

Urrea, José. Diary. In *The Mexican Side of the Texas Revolution*, translated by Carlos E. Castaneda. Dallas: P. L. Turner Company, 1928.

Walraven, Bill and Marjorie. *The Magnificent Barbarians*. Austin: Eakin Press, 1993.

Wharton, Clarence. *Remember Goliad*. Glorietta, New Mexico: The Rio Grande Press, Inc., 1968.

Williams, Amelia W., and Eugene C. Barker, eds. *The Writings of Sam*

Houston, 1813-1863. 8 vols. Austin: University of Texas Press, 1938-43.

Wisehart, M. K. *Sam Houston: American Giant.* Washington: Robert B. Luce, Inc., 1962.

Yoakum, Henderson. *History of Texas, From Its First Settlement in 1685 to Its Annexation to the United States in 1846.* 2 vols. New York: J. S. Redfield, 1855.

ARTICLES

Barker, Eugene C. "The Tampico Expedition." *Texas Historical Association Quarterly,* Vol. 6, January 1903.

————."The Texan Revolutionary Army." *Texas Historical Association Quarterly,* Vol. 9, April 1906.

Foote, Henry Stuart. "Texas and the Texans." *Southwestern Historical Quarterly,* Vol. 2, July 1898 to April 1899.

Davenport, Harbert. "The Men of Goliad!" *Southwestern Historical Quarterly,* Vol. 43, July 1939.

Smith, Ruth Cumby. "James W. Fannin, Jr., in the Texas Revolution." *Southwestern Historical Quarterly,* Vol. 23, October 1919.

MANUSCRIPT COLLECTIONS

Center for American History, University of Texas, Austin, Texas. Stephen F. Austin Papers, Vol. 3.

Texas State Archives.

NEWSPAPERS

The Colorado Gazette and Advertiser, January 25, 1840.

Telegraph and Texas Register, March 24, 1836.

PERIODICALS

The Alamo Long Barrack Museum, compiled by the Daughters of the Republic of Texas, San Antonio, 1986.

MEMOIRS

Sabina Brown Memoirs.

INDEX

A

Adams, John, 122
Advisory Committee, 57
Agua Dulce Creek, x, 44, 53-54, 82, 86, 89, 124, 130, 131
Alabama Greys, 43, 45, 88
Alabama Red Rovers, 44, 48, 97, 100, 112, 120, 123, 125, 149
Alabama volunteers, 46, 88
Alamo, 20-21, 29, 34-35, 36, 38, 41, 59-63, 143
Alamo, Battle of the, x, xi, 64-76, 82, 83, 95, 127
Alavez, Francita, 54, 115, 124, 126, 148-149
    Telesforo, 124, 148-149
Alazan Hill, 64
Alcerrica, Augustin, 120
Aldama Battalion, 70
Allen, John M., 41
Almonte, Juan Nepomuceno, 65, 70, 71, 95
Amador, Juan Valentin, 71, 74
Amat, Augustin, 70, 71, 74
Anahuac, 2-3, 35, 77
Andrade, Juan José, 33, 76, 77, 127
Angel of Goliad, 54, 126, 148-149
Apaches, 37
Aransas Bay, 5
Archer, Branch T., 12
Arroyo de las Ratas, 85
Aurora, 47
Austin, John, 3
    Moses, 10

Stephen F., vii, 5, 6, 7, 9-10, 11, 12, 17, 18, 19, 24, 147-148
Ayers, David, 72, 92-93
    Lewis, 46, 86-87
    Mrs., 93

B

Balderas, Luis, 120
Bara, D. N., 114-115
Barker, Eugene C., 108-109
Barnard, Dr. Joseph Henry, 46, 47-49, 62-63, 80, 96, 102-103, 106, 107, 108, 112-113, 114, 118, 119-120, 125, 127-128, 149
Barnet, Col., 59
Bay Prairie, 6
Baylor University, 150
Belton, Francis S., 16
Ben (Almonte's servant), 95
Benavides, Placido, x, 54
Bennet, Valentine, 46
Bexar, Battle of, x
Bexar road, 120
Blanco, ———, 88-89
Bonham, James Butler, 42, 66, 72, 75, 146
Bower, John White, 46
Bowie, James, x, 10-12, 20, 21, 22, 28, 29, 34-35, 36, 55, 59, 65, 72, 75, 76, 95, 144, 146
    Ursula de Veramendi, 76
Bowie knife, 55
Bowles, Chief, 34
Bradburn, John, 2-4
Bradford, Benjamin F., 45, 88

Brazos Guards, 11, 17
Breece, Thomas, 42
Brister, Nathaniel R., 46
Brooks, John Sowers, 46, 50, 60, 80,
    84
    Mary Ann, 80
Brown, Reuben, 54, 124
    Sabina, 86-87, 88
    Samuel T., 123
Brutus, 48
Buena Vista, Battle of, 148
Buffalo Bayou, xi, 141, 143
Bullock, Munroe, 92
    Uriah J., 43
Burke, David N., 42, 45
Burleson, Edward, 11, 20, 21, 23, 43,
    79, 83
Burnham's crossing, 95
Bustamante, Anastasio, viii
Bustamante's law, viii, ix, 2
Byars, Noah, 67

C
Cameron, Verne, 69, 82
Campeachy Indians, 103
Cara, Ramon Martínez, 117
Carajabal, Mariana, x
Caroline, 39, 40, 55
Cash, Mrs., 104
Cassiano, José, x
Castaneda, Francisco, 4
Castrillon, Manuel Fernandez, 70,
    74, 75
Catholicism, vii
Chadwick, Joseph March, 46, 49,
    109, 118
Chenoweth, John, 41
Cherokees, 3, 14, 28, 31, 34
Claiborne, Alabama, 35
Clements, 59
Coahuila-Texas, vii, viii, 1, 10, 23
Cole, Everett, 110
Coleto Battlefield Monument, xii,
    140, 149, 151
Coleto Creek, 99
Coleto Plains, Battle of, vii, xi, 1,
    100, 101-110, 129, 149
Collinsworth, George Morse, 6-7, 50

James, 84
Colorado River, 95, 122, 127
Comanches, 37
"Come and Take It" cannon, 4
Commitee of Safety, 4, 5
Concepción, Battle of, x, xi, 11
Constitution of 1824, vii-viii, ix, 8,
    79
Consultation, 9, 10, 13, 16
Convention, 67-68, 72, 79, 82
Cooke, William G., 42, 43, 45, 150
Copano, 23, 24, 41, 57, 58, 93
Copano Bay, 5, 114, 119
Copano road, 93
Cós, Martín Perfecto de, 5, 6, 10-12,
    18, 20, 22, 23, 33, 51, 66, 70,
    71, 74
Cox's Point, 40, 55, 62
Creek Indians, 13
Crockett, Davy, ix, 35, 59, 75, 95,
    146
Cruz y Arocha, Antonio, x
Cuautla Regiment, 115
Cuellar, Jesus "Comanche," 20, 85
    Salvador, 85
Cummings, Rebecca, 72

D
Davenport, Harbert, 129
de la Garza, Alejandro, x
    Carlos, 91-92
de la luz Gonzales, Jose, 107
de la Pena, José Enrique, 36, 53, 65,
    66, 70, 143, 144
de la Vara, Rafael, 93
de Sprain, Randolph, 54
Declaration of Independence,
    Dimitt's, 8
Declaration of Independence, Texas,
    ix, x, 83
Delawares, 34
Desauque, Francis J., 83, 107, 112
Desiderio Hill, 38
Dickinson, Almeron, 75
    Angelina, 75, 95
    Susannah, 75, 95
Dimitt, Philip, 7, 8, 21-23, 24, 28,
    150

Dimitt's Landing, 29, 55, 62
Duque, Francisco, 70, 74
Duval, Burr H., 39, 44, 45, 49, 80-
    81, 100, 122, 151
    John Crittenden, 56, 122, 151
Duval's Mustangs, 45
Early Times in Texas*, 56
Edwards brothers, ix
Ehrenberg, Herman, 53, 63, 99, 104,
    105, 113, 121-122, 150
Ellis, Richard, 68, 72
Emeline, 39, 40
Esparza, Francisco, 76
    Gregorio, 76
    Mrs. Gregorio, 75-76
Espiritu Santo Bay, 48

F
Fannin County, 151
Fannin, Isham, 15
    James Walker, Jr.: abandons Fort
        Defiance, 98-99; appointed
        agent of Prov. Govt., 25, 27, 30;
        appointed colonel, 14, 19, 144;
        appointed inspector general, 14,
        19; in Battle of Coleto Plains,
        100, 101-110; in Battle of
        Concepción, 11; in Battle of
        Gonzales, 17; birth of, 15; burial
        of, 128; as commander at La
        Bahía, ix, 40-46, 47, 48, 49-51,
        55-63, 77-81, 82-89, 92, 96, 98,
        129, 143, 145; county named
        for, 151; executed, vii, 125, 145;
        in illegal slave trade, 15-16;
        indecisiveness of, 57, 58-59, 61,
        78, 85, 86, 145; loss of men
        under, 119-140, 141, 145; and
        Matamoros Expedition, 22, 39-
        40, 55, 56, 79; at military acade-
        my, 15, 19; as prisoner, 111-118;
        response to Alamo appeals, 59-
        63, 72, 77, 145; response to
        Houston's order, 82-89, 96, 98,
        144; self-assessment of, 57, 59,
        80; sugar plantation of, 16, 61;
        surrenders, xi, 106-110; town
        named for, 151; wounded, 103

Minerva, 15, 151
    Pinckney, 151
Fannin, Texas, 151
Field, Joseph E., 112, 114, 119, 126-
    127
Filisola, Vicente, 33, 37, 76, 77, 128,
    142, 150
flag, Dimitt's, 8
flag, Texas, 79
Forbes, John, 31, 34
Fort Defiance, vii, 50, 55, 77, 78, 83,
    86, 88, 96, 97, 98, 100, 118,
    128, 140, 145
Frazer, Hugh McDonald, 44, 46, 96-
    97, 112, 149
Fredonia, Republic of, ix
Fredonian Rebellion, ix
Fuller, Edward, 45

G
Gaono, Antonio, 33, 76, 77
Garay, Francisco, 85, 91 92, 100,
    119-120, 126
Garcitas Creek, 48
Gatlin, William J., 54
General Council, 12, 13, 14, 19, 24-
    25, 27, 28, 30, 31, 36, 44, 47,
    56, 60, 79
Georgia Battalion, 39, 43-44, 45, 93,
    96, 123
Georgia Rattlers, 88, 92, 93, 126
Georgia volunteers, 46
German volunteers, 46
Goliad, 2, 5, 20, 27, 28, 31, 33, 40,
    41-46, 51, 55-63, 66, 77, 82, 83-
    86, 100, 127, 128, 134-140, 151
Goliad executions, 134-138, 141-142
Goliad Massacre, 110
Goliad, monument at, xii, 140, 149,
    151
Goliad road, 7, 104
Gonzales, x, 4, 17, 47, 65, 77, 78,
    83, 96, 121, 143, 32
"Gonzales 32," 66, 68, 69, 72, 143
Gonzales, Battle of, xi, 17
Gonzales, Petra, 76
Grace, John C., 44, 45
Grant, James, x, 23-25, 26, 27, 28,

30, 33-34, 40, 42, 43, 44, 51,
  52-54, 82, 86, 89, 124, 130, 131
Greys, 105, 120, 121, *also see* New
  Orleans Greys; San Antonio
  Greys
Grimes, Jesse, 72
Guadalupe River, 98, 123, 127
Guerra, Luis, 39, 45-46, 79-80, 88-
  89
Guerrero, 33
Guerrero, José Maria (Brigido), 76

H
Hale, Dr., 114
Hamilton, Isaac D., 98, 123-124
Handy, Nancy N., 149
Hanrick, Edward, 43
Hart, Captain, 39
Hays, Jack, 151
Hill, Mrs., 86
Hitchcock, A. J., 133
Hockley, George, 28, 31, 34, 69
Holland, Benjamin H., 46
Holliday, John, 123
Holsinger, Juan José, 91, 107, 108,
  109, 113, 118, 122, 126, 132,
  142
Holt, David, 46
Horseshoe Bend, Battle of, 13
Horton, Albert Clinton, 40, 42, 44,
  69, 84, 90, 97-98, 99, 101-102,
  133, 150
Houston, Sam, x, 4-5, 9-10, 13-15,
  18, 19, 21, 22, 23, 25, 26, 27,
  28-31, 34, 35, 45, 50, 56, 57, 59,
  65, 67-69, 75, 79, 82-84, 86, 95,
  96, 98, 121, 141, 143, 144, 147,
  148, 149
Hughes, Benjamin F., 126
Hurst, Stephen D., 46
Huson, Hobart, 48

I
Invincible, 39

J
Jack, William H., 151
Jackson, Andrew, 13

Jameson, Green B., 64
Jiminez Battalion, 71, 105
Joe (Travis' slave), 75, 95
John (Bowie's slave), 75
Johnson,——, 111
  Francis W., 3, 21, 23, 24-25, 26,
    27, 28, 30, 33-34, 40, 42, 43, 44,
    51, 52-53, 54, 60, 61, 82, 86, 89,
    129, 130, 149

K
Karnes, Henry, 95
Kentucky volunteers, 45, 46, 81, 83,
  86
Kerr,——, 59
  James, 6
Kickapoos, 34
King, Amon Butler, 41, 44, 45, 60,
  86-89, 90-92, 96, 97, 131, 145

L
La Bahía, vii, 5, 6, 7, 8, 40, 41-46,
  48-50, 55-63, 111, 113, 116,
  128, 151
La Bahía road, 69, 91, 92
Lafayette Battalion, 45
Lamar, Mirabeau B., 43, 122, 147,
  150
Laredo, 32
Laredo road, 18
Lavaca Bay, 52
Lavaca River, 48, 93
Lawrence, Benjamin L., 42, 45
Lewellen, Thomas, 43
Liberty road, 3
Linn, John L., 8
Lipantitlan, 7
Long, Dr. James, ix
Long Expedition, ix, 6, 10
Lopez ranch, 86-87, 89
Los Leoncitos, 11
Louisiana volunteers, 46
Louisville Journal, 124
Louisville volunteers, 42
Love, Hugh, 34
Lynch's Ferry, 77

M
Magee, Augustus William, 49
Magee-Gutierrez Expedition, ix, 49
Manahuilla Creek, 99, 112
Martin, Albert, 69
Martínez,——, 120
Mary Jane, 22
Maryland volunteers, 46
Matagorda, 6, 19-20, 28, 47, 62, 122
Matagorda Bay, 78
Matagorda volunteers, 44
Matamoros Battalion, 71
Matamoros Expedition, 21-31, 33-
    34, 39-40, 42, 43, 47, 51, 52-54,
    55, 64, 79, 149
Matamoros, Mexico, 21-22, 57, 58,
    66, 130
Mattawamkeag, 39, 40
McCullough, Sam, 7
McMonomy, J. B., 45
Men of Goliad, The, 129
Menefee's settlement, 6
Mercer's settlement, 6
Merifield, J. Q., 56
Mexia, José Antonio, 22-23, 80
Mexican army, 33, 37, 40, 60, 64-67,
    70-71, 73-76, 89, 102, 105-106,
    109, 127
Milam, Benjamin R., 6, 7, 11, 20-21,
    144, 146
Military Affairs Committee, 14, 19,
    84
militia, 13, 14, 56, 58, 69
Miller, William C., 114-115, 117,
    119, 124, 125, 127
Mims, Joseph, 16, 61
Minerva Fort, 151
Miracle, Pedro Julian, 22
Mission Concepción, 11, 65
Mission Espada, 70
Mission Espiritu Santo de Zuniga,
    40, 97
Mission River, 86, 87
Mississippi volunteers, 43, 46
Mitchell, Warren J., 41, 90, 115
Mobile Greys, 42, 45
Monclova, 33
Moore,——, 101

John H., 4
Mora, Ventura, 65
Morales, Juan 64, 71, 74, 77, 97,
    100, 107, 109
Morris, Robert C., 21, 28, 30, 39-40,
    42, 43, 53
Moses, David, 54, 86
Murphy, James, 92
Mustang company, 42, 45, 56, 100

N
Nacogdoches, 2, 3, 4, 34, 77
Nacogdoches Department, 4
Napoleon, 143
Navarro, Angela, 150
    José Antonio, x, 150
Neill, James C., 21, 26, 28, 29, 30,
    34-35, 36, 42, 83
New Orleans Greys, 5, 21, 28, 29,
    42, 45, 51-52, 55, 100
New York *Evening Star*, 125
New York volunteers, 46
Nuestra Señora de Purisima
    Concepción de Acuna, 10-11
Nunez, Gabriel, 91, 100, 103

O
Oak Grove, 100
Ohio volunteers, 46, 83

P
Parker, Isaac, 4
Parras, Mexico, 24
Paso Cavallo, 42
Peace Party, 12
Peach Tree Village, 31, 34
Pearson, Thomas K., 29, 30, 42, 61
Perdido Creek, 100
Perry, Edward, 92
Petrussewicz, H. Francis, 46, 103
Pettus, Samuel Overton, 45, 112
Piedras, José de la, 3-4
Poe, George W., 26
Polish volunteers, 46, 50, 103
Port Lavaca, 55
Portilla, José Nicolas de la, 111, 116-
    117, 125
Potter, Robert, 68

Pretalia, Rafael, 89, 90, 115
Provisional Government, 8, 9-10, 12, 144, 148
Pruett, Jakie, 110

R
Ramirez, Antonio, 120
Rangers, 12-13, 36, 69, also see Texas Rangers
Reed, James, 54
Refugio, 28, 29, 31, 39, 86-89, 90-91, 92, 96, 131, 145
Refugio Militia Company, 44, 46
Refugio, monument at, 131
Refugio road, 85, 120
Refugio volunteers, 7
Republic of the Rio Grande, 24
Rios,——, 87
Ripley, Harry, 103-104
Robinson, James W., 12, 27, 48, 50, 56, 58, 59, 60, 64, 78, 79, 144, 148
Romero, José Maria, 64, 70, 71, 74
Rose, Gideon, 46
    Louis, 72
Rosenbury,——, 125
Ruiz, Francisco Antonio, x, 76
    José Francisco, x
Runaway Scrape, 86, 121
Rusk, Polly, 148
    Thomas Jefferson, 35, 128, 147, 148, 151

S
Sabine River, 77
Salado Creek, 9
Salas, Mariano, 70, 100, 109
San Antonio, Battle of, xi
San Antonio de Bexar, 2, 5, 10, 18, 26, 27, 29, 30, 35, 36-38, 47, 57, 60, 61, 69
San Antonio Greys, 42, 45
San Antonio River, 10, 48, 62, 97, 98, 111, 112, 115, 120, 121, 127
San Antonio, siege of, 20-21
San Bernard River, 16
San Felipe de Austin, 9, 10, 12, 14, 35, 56

San Fernando church, 38, 66
San Jacinto, Battle of, xi, 122, 127, 141, 147, 148, 149, 150
San Luis Potosi, 33
San Luis regiment, 70
San Patricio, 43, 44, 51, 52-53, 54, 57, 82, 85, 89
Sandoval, Lieutenant Colonel, 7
Santa Anna, Antonio López de, vii, 1-2, 20, 24, 32-33, 36-38, 45, 51, 64-67, 69-71, 73-77, 82, 84, 85, 93, 116-117, 120, 122, 127, 141-144, 148, 150
Santa Anna's Campaign Against Texas, 1835-1836, 71
Santos, Richard G., 36, 71
Saucedo, Trinidad, 76
Saunders, B. F., 41
Savariego, D. N., 117
Scurlock, William, 54
Scurry, Richardson, 69
Seguin, Juan Nepomuceno, x, 26, 38
Sesma, Joaquin Ramirez y, 32-33, 37, 64, 69-70, 77, 95, 96
Shackelford, Dr. John (Jack), 1, 44, 46, 48, 96, 97, 99-100, 101-102, 106, 107, 108, 112, 114, 119-120, 123, 125, 126, 127-128, 149
Shawnees, 3, 34
Sherman, Sidney, 83
Simpson,——, 93
Smith, Deaf, 95, 96
    Henry, 12, 17, 19, 22, 25, 27, 28, 29, 30, 31, 34, 36, 47, 50, 64, 144
    John W., 38, 69, 72
    Ruth Cumby, 80, 84
Spohn, Joseph H., 1, 125
Sprague, Samuel, 44
St. John, Samuel P., 42
State Cemetery, 151
Sterne, Adolphus, 5
Sutherland, John, 38

T
Tamaulipas, 39, 40
Tampico, 79

Tampico Blues, 22
Tampico Expedition, 22-23, 41, 88
Tampico regiment, 45-46, 102
Tarleton, James, 42
Tennessee volunteers, 46
Texas army, 12-13, 19, 20, 21, 25,
    26, 30, 34, 40, 41-46, 47, 49,
    50-51, 53, 58, 59, 60, 68, 79, 81,
    82, 83, 95-96, 104-105, 128,
    141, 143, 147, 148, 149
Texas Rangers, 151
Texas Und Seine Revolution, 151
Thompson, Mr., 16
Thornton, Francis S., 41
Ticknor, Isaac, 43, 88, 115
Tolsa, Eugenio, 33, 77
Toluca Battalion, 70
Tornel, José Maria, 32
Travis, Charles, 72
    Rosanna, 35
    William Barret, x, 2-3, 19, 28, 30,
        35-36, 38, 47, 59, 61, 64-65, 66-
        67, 68, 71-72, 75, 95, 143, 144,
        145, 146,
Treadway, Capt., 53
Tres Villas, 113
Turner, Captain, 39, 40
Turtle Bayou, 3

U
Ugartechea, Domingo de, 3, 127
Urizza, Fernando, 75
Urrea, José, 33-34, 40, 51, 52-54, 58,
    63, 77, 84, 85, 87, 89, 90-94, 96,
    97, 98, 100, 101-110, 111, 112,
    115-116, 117, 122, 132, 142,
    145

V
Velasco, 2, 3, 26, 27, 127
Veramendi, Don Juan Martín de, x,
    10, 21
    Ursula, 10, *also see* Bowie, Ursula

Victoria, 44, 78, 83-84, 96, 98, 128,
    132-133
Victoria road, 104, 120, 121
Victorian Guards, 91-92
Voss,———, 126-127

W
Wadsworth, William A. O., 43
Walker, James F., 15
    James W., 15
Wallace, Benjamin C., 45, 106-107,
    109
    Big-Foot, 151
War Party, 35
Ward, William, 29-30, 41, 43, 60, 88,
    90, 92, 93, 96, 115-116, 123,
    126, 131, 132, 145
Washington-on-the-Brazos, 13, 27,
    67, 72
West Point, 15, 17, 19
Western Army, 5
Westmore, 45
Westover, Ira J., 7, 40, 41, 58, 61
Wharton, John A., 142
    William H., 12
White,———, 125
Wiggington, H. R. A., 42, 45
Williamson, R. M., 69
Winn, James C., 43
With Milam and Fannin in Texas, 105
Woll, Adrian, 148
Wood,———, 93
Wood, James, 124
Wyatt, Peyton S., 41, 44, 45, 140

Y
Yucatan Indians, 92

Z
Zacatecas, 2
Zavala, Lorenzo de, x

About the Author

Clifford Hopewell was born in Dallas, where he attended Southern Methodist University and studied fiction and article writing.

During World War II Hopewell was a navigator on a B-17 Flying Fortress and was stationed with the 94th Bomb Group in England. While bombing Emden, Germany, in May 1943, his aircraft blew up. One of two survivors of the ten-man crew, he subsequently spent two years in a prisoner-of-war camp for Allied Air Force officers at Stalag Luft III near Sagan, Germany.

Reverting to civilian life after the war, he was recalled to service during the Korean War and served for thirteen months.

A retired life insurance agent, Hopewell for some years has been writing articles for newspapers and magazines. He is the author of *Jim Bowie: Texas Fighting Man*, *Sam Houston: Man of Destiny*, and *Combine 13*, an account of his two years as a prisoner of war.

Still residing in Dallas, Hopewell is married and has two sons and several grandchildren.